Consumer Protection in E-Retailing in ASEAN

Consumer Protection in E-Retailing in ASEAN

Huong Ha

BEP

BUSINESS EXPERT PRESS

Leader in applied, concise business books

First published in 2021 by
Business Expert Press, LLC
222 East 46th Street, New York, NY 10017
www.businessexpertpress.com

ISBN-13: 978-1-95334-960-6 (paperback)
ISBN-13: 978-1-95334-961-3 (e-book)

Business Expert Press Business Law and Corporate Risk Management Collection

Collection ISSN: 2333-6722 (print)
Collection ISSN: 2333-6730 (electronic)

First edition: 2021

10 9 8 7 6 5 4 3 2 1

Description

While many sectors and industries have been badly affected by the COVID-19 pandemic, e-retailing is one of the booming sectors during this period. Even before the global pandemic, the e-retailing sector was already booming with the online retail sales being forecasted to reach several trillions by 2023. Although e-retailing offers many opportunities for businesses and consumers, there are several issues associated with e-consumer protection, that is, consumers face various types of risk, such as insufficient information about transactions, unsecured online payment modes, privacy and security, inaccessible redress mechanism, goods not delivered, or defective goods received.

This book aims to examine how consumers are protected on the online marketplace in the context of ASEAN countries, and what are the challenges of e-consumer protection in the digital era. Specifically, this project aims to:

(i) Discuss the six issues of e-consumer protection, including issues associated with information about transaction, product quality, privacy, security, redress, and jurisdiction.

(ii) Examine the policy/governance approach adopted by the public sector, the private sector, and the third sector to address the issues associated with e-consumer protection.

(iii) Propose a multisector governance framework for e-consumer protection.

Three short case studies on Lazada in Singapore, Shopee in Vietnam, and Zalora in Malaysia are included to illustrate how well-known e-retailers protect their e-customers. This book aims to provide sources of information and knowledge which focus on both theoretical and practical aspects of e-consumer protection. The book is significant for the following reasons. First, it is interdisciplinary in nature, including research on consumer protection, governance, management, and policy/regulation. Second, the views from different groups of stakeholders in different sectors are incorporated in the discussion in order to produce comprehensive findings and analysis of the governance and management process, best practices, and implementation to address issues associated with e-consumer protection. Finally, the proposed book presents research on e-consumer protection in different countries in ASEAN.

Keywords

e-consumer protection; multisector governance; e-retailing; e-retailers; industry association; information disclosure; self-regulation; privacy; security; redress; jurisdiction; ASEAN

Contents

List of Figures

List of Tables

Foreword

In 2006, I bought a new motorcycle for U.S.$10,000, sight unseen except on the Internet, by credit card purchase from a dealer I had never visited located in a city 2,420 miles from my home. I hadn't ridden a motorcycle in 33 years and it was a dangerous thing to do. The main danger lay in the e-retailing transaction rather than the cross-country motorcycle trip that followed. This was my first experience of substantial magnitude with e-commerce.

So much could have gone wrong. I had no basis for judging whether the dealer was honest or might use my credit card information for nefarious purposes. Perhaps, the information would be taken by hackers to run up a number of purchases before the credit card was shut down. Knowing that I would be away from home, the dealer, near the U.S. west coast, could have targeted my empty house for burglary by accomplices on the east coast. He could have given or sold my credit card information to others and I could have become a victim of identity theft. He might have withheld knowledge that the motorcycle had significant defects or claimed that it did and charged me for (un)necessary repairs. Because the motorcycle was from Japan I might have had no recourse. The defects could have occurred in manufacturing, in shipping, or at the dealer's shop during assembly and preparation. Even if all went well, which it did, I might still have been disappointed because the Internet information I used in deciding to buy the motorcycle was false or misleading.

E-retailing has come a long way since 2006. Its benefits to consumers—convenience, choice, price, and the ease of comparing multiple sellers—are substantial and enable some e-retailers, such as Amazon in the United States, to thrive almost beyond imagination. E-retailing also promotes local, regional, and national economic growth, though often at a significant cost to brick and mortar commerce. But many of the pitfalls remain similar. The old aphorism, "Never buy a pig in a poke," is still apt. When making e-retail purchases, consumers cannot use their five senses as they might in assessing products in a conventional store or marketplace. They cannot try on our out what they are buying. Neither can they make personal assessments of the sellers' honesty the way they might in face-to-face interactions with them. Caveat emptor remains critical.

The main purpose of this wonderfully informative and insightful book is to improve e-retailing, especially from the consumers' perspectives. Much of the focus is on ASEAN nations, which provides very valuable comparative analysis. The book consists of six succinct, yet comprehensive chapters including an introduction and conclusion. These cover the overall "issues associated with e-consumer protection," "the current governance framework for e-consumer protection," "a proposed governance framework for e-consumer protection," and three case studies drawn on experiences in Singapore, Vietnam, and Malaysia followed by a conclusion drawing the entire book together.

Chapter 1 introduces the subject matter by defining e-retailing and outlining its advantages and disadvantages, e-consumer rights and protections, and governance for e-consumer protection.

Chapter 2 discusses the main problems associated with e-retailing. These include deceptive advertising, guarantee and warranty, unauthorized billing, late or non-delivery of products, wrong product delivery, shipping costs, poor quality of products and services, unclear price and payment, unclear terms and conditions, lack of information about redress, misleading information, security and privacy along with refunds, exchanges, and other redress, especially in cross-border transactions under different legal regimes. Additionally, as the chapter explains there are the collateral risks posed by exposure of personal and financial information by sophisticated schemes for phishing, pharming, smishing, vishing, breaching privacy, spam, spim, spyware, and the like.

Chapter 3 analyzes efforts to regulate e-retailing through a variety of approaches at the national, regional, and international levels. The chapter explains that both overregulation and underregulation are problematic and, accordingly, a complex balance of measures is necessary. Importantly, the chapter emphasizes how different nations adopt different balances and that compliance with guidelines and mandatory regulations is variable and cannot be assumed.

Chapter 4 is among the major contributions of this excellent book. It develops a proposed model of governance of e-retailing for improving consumer protection. Based on responsiveness, transparency, participation and inclusion, consulting and consensus building, and accountability—standard good governance criteria—this model beneficially adds e-consumer involvement to the extant structure of regulation by government, e-retailing businesses, and civil society organizations. The book contends "that e-consumers should be treated as a distinct sector in the governance framework to address e-consumer protection according to the principle of participation" because as "key actors in e-retailing, it is highly undesirable to omit them from any activities and programs which affect their well-being." E-consumers' roles in the proposed model include developing greater knowledge of how e-retailing operates, their rights, and their social responsibilities for improving it. The reality is that, collectively, e-consumers are the driving force of e-retailing; without them, it could not exist and, therefore, they are in a position to shape its existence.

Chapter 5 grounds and expands much of the foregoing analysis in case studies of e-retailing by Lazada, Shopee, and Zalora. *Chapter 6* admirably brings the entire book together and calls for future research testing the proposed framework, exploring the role of media in improving e-retailing and e-consumer knowledge, and gaining a greater understanding of e-consumer behavior, especially with regard to protecting their own interests.

As the book explains, "many e-consumers may not practice sufficient self-protection when shopping online due to lack of awareness of online risk." I was clearly in that category when I bought my motorcycle many years ago and thereafter. As with others who read this highly readable, enjoyable, and insightful book, I will never be in that category again. The more widely this outstanding book is read, the better e-retailing and the protection of e-consumers will be.

David H. Rosenbloom
Distinguished Professor of Public Administration and
Editor-in-Chief, Routledge Public Administration
and Public Policy Series
Department of Public Administration and Policy
School of Public Affairs
American University
Washington, DC, USA

Acknowledgments

It was impossible to complete this book without the support of my family members and friends. I take pride in acknowledging the exceptional and tireless support of Dr. Stanley Bruce Thomson during the review and proofreading process and Prof. David H. Rosenbloom for his great support and the foreword. My great appreciation goes to Dr. Thomson and Prof. Rosenbloom as always. Finally, I am very grateful for the advice and assistance from the series editor/s of BEP, USA.

Associate Professor Huong Ha
School of Business, Singapore University of Social Sciences
Singapore

CHAPTER 1

Introduction of E-Consumer Protection in E-Retailing in ASEAN

Introduction

This book investigates the issues associated with consumer protection in e-retailing (or e-consumer protection). It also examines the roles of e-retailers, government, industry, and consumer associations in the current policy framework for e-consumer protection, and cooperation among groups of stakeholders. In addition, this book proposes a multisector governance framework with e-consumers as one of the main sectors.

This book consists of four chapters excluding the introduction and the conclusion. An overview of each chapter is presented here. Chapter 2 examines six issues associated with e-consumer protection, such as (i) information disclosure, (ii) product quality, (iii) security, (iv) privacy, (v) redress, and (vi) jurisdiction. Chapter 3 discusses the current policy framework for e-consumer protection, highlighting the roles of the public sector (government or the state), the private sector (business or e-retailers), and civil society (the third sector or civil society organizations). Chapter 4 outlines the weaknesses of the current governance framework for protecting e-consumers and proposes a four-sector governance model to enhance e-consumer protection. Chapter 5 illustrates how e-retailers protect their e-consumers in the real life by examining three e-retailers, namely Lazada in Singapore, Shopee in Vietnam, and Zalora in Malaysia.

Specifically, this introduction chapter discusses various concepts pertaining to e-retailing and business transactions. It also explains the advantages and disadvantages of shopping online. Consumer rights and consumer protection are elaborated in the next section, followed by a brief explanation of governance and e-consumer protection.

E-Retailing

Concept of E-Retailing

The definition of e-retailing (electronic retailing) is important because it helps us decide which transactions are e-transactions. It can thus help us identify the distinctive features of e-retailing and traditional commerce. This, in turn, allows the comparison and contrast of the attributes of customer protection in both online and offline marketplaces. In practice, e-retailing, e-commerce, and e-business have been used interchangeably although there are differences among these modes of commerce.

The continuous and rapid evolution of e-retailing in the context of political, socioeconomic, and technological changes, consumer demand for new products (goods and services) and processes, changes in business practices in terms of customer–supplier relationship, payment mechanisms, and implementation of advanced technological applications creates difficulties in finding a comprehensive and common definition for e-retailing (Weill and Vitale 2001; Ha 2012, 2013, 2017). Several definitions are used by different organizations. For example, e-retailing is defined as:

> consumer-facing e-commerce transaction ... excludes online job search services, financial services and billing services. (Dobbs et al. 2013, p. 1)

Weill and Vitale (2001) propose particular elements of an e-business, including

> marketing, buying, selling, delivering, servicing, and paying for products, services, and information. (p. 5)

The OECD (2002) offers a broader definition of e-commerce that is also applicable to e-retailing:

> the sale or purchase of goods and services, whether between businesses and households, individuals, governments, or other public and private organizations, conducted over the computer-mediated

networks. The goods and services are ordered over those networks, but the payment and the ultimate deliver of the good and service may be conducted on or off-line. (p. 89)

The OECD definition is more comprehensive than other definitions in that it clearly includes the mode of conduct for transactions (over computer-mediated networks) and the modes of payment and delivery of goods and services (online or offline). Goods refers to any tangible products, whereas services include "messaging and a variety of services" which enable the searching, dissemination, and delivery of information as well as "negotiation, transaction, and settlement" (Rahman 2000, p. 5).

From the consumers' perspective, business transactions include three main stages, namely (i) *pretransaction* (e.g., collection of information about goods and services, prices, features/specifications, terms and conditions, business name, address and contact, sales and promotion, information from other e-retailers for comparison); (ii) *transaction* (e.g., the order, negotiation, and agreement on the terms and conditions, transacted prices, the mode of payment and delivery), and (iii) *posttransaction* (e.g., the receipt of goods and services, the requests for a refund, an exchange, or after-sales services, such as guarantee, warranty, maintenance, repair, and sending complaints or compliments to e-retailers) (Fergusson 2000; Ha 2017; Ha and Coghill 2008).

In traditional commerce, all three stages are conducted in a physical marketplace. In e-retailing, the first two stages are usually done online, whereas the delivery in the third stage can be executed both online and offline, depending on the nature of goods/services purchased. Hence, according to the OECD (2002) definition, the basic difference between online and offline transactions is exhibited in all three stages. And the OECD definition is adopted for discussion in this volume.

Advantages and Disadvantages of E-Retailing

E-retailing has offered several benefits to users, such as speed, convenience, availability (i.e., 24 hours per day, 7 days a week), flexibility, and available information about goods and services online and reduction of costs to search for information (Doolin et al. 2005; Kim and Lennon 2012;

Kita et al. 2018; Lokken et al. 2003). A survey in the United States in April 2020 revealed that 51 percent and 21 percent of the respondents explained that price and fast and convenient delivery affected their decisions to shop online (Clement 2020). E-consumers are able to select from a wide range of products and services, goods and services can be purchased at a better price, and communication between e-consumers and e-retailers is faster (Hui and Wan 2007). E-consumers can also avoid discrimination based on religion, gender, and other factors (Alboukrek 2003). E-consumers can browse and purchase products online via different channels and devices (laptops, desktops, tablets, phones) (Wagner, Schramm-Klein and Steinman 2020). Additionally, from a macro-economic view, e-consumers can "capture a much larger fraction of the surplus created by the online distribution channel than firms" (Duch-brown et al. 2017, para. 67).

However, many factors have deterred Internet users from shopping online, including deceptive advertising, guarantee and warranty, unauthorized billing, late or nondelivery of products, wrong product delivery, shipping costs, poor quality of products and services, unclear price and payment, unclear terms and conditions, lack of information about redress, misleading information, and security and privacy (Aïmeur, Lawani and Dalkir 2016; Aragoncillo and Orús 2018; Invest Northern Ireland undated; Kaushik et al. 2020; Oliveira et al. 2017; WTO 2020). The recent COVID-19 pandemic has also entailed many supply chain bottlenecks of online purchases and delivery of goods (WTO 2020). This issue has grown bigger due to new health regulations and travel restrictions that have disrupted international transport and logistics services (WTO 2020). Other factors that discourage Internet users to shop online include the need to touch, feel, see, and try a product and to talk to a salesperson before purchasing (Mann and Liu-Thompkins 2019). Also, e-consumers also worry about difficulties in refund and exchange when purchasing goods online (Consumer Affairs Victoria 2003, 2004; Lokken et al. 2003).

In addition, since e-consumer trust is essential for e-retailers to drive consumer e-transactions (Lin, Wang and Hajli 2019), practices of unscrupulous e-retailers and other cyber threats have eroded e-consumer trust and confidence in e-retailing (Deloitte 2015). According to Deloitte (2015), e-consumers are more active now, and 73 percent of consumers would not engage with a company if the company did not keep their data safe and confidential. Also, given the rapid development and adoption of advanced technology, and the cross-border nature of e-retailing, e-consumers are also worried about insecure e-transactions (Huia and Wan 2007). Many difficulties regarding governance, such as applicable laws and regulations, the enforcement of local laws in another jurisdiction, and cross-border activities have also arisen (e.g., how to ensure that goods and services can meet international standards of health and safety). The situation is worse when there has been an increase in the number of complaints associated with e-retailing, especially during the COVID-19 pandemic and cross-border e-transactions (Fletcher 2020; WTO 2020). Greene (2020) stated that customers of Amazon in the United States were very frustrated with e-sellers during the COVID-19 lockdown, and more than 11 percent of reviews of e-sellers were negative in the past one month. Further, e-consumers are less likely to purchase online if they perceived there is a higher level of risk, such as "performance risk (i.e., low product quality), psychological risk (i.e., mental discomfort), financial risk (monetary loss), and payment risks (i.e., information misuse)" (Lin et al 2019, p. 331).

Thus, there is a need to examine the attitudes of e-consumers toward these factors and whether there are emerging risks and threats in e-retailing. Another question is how and by whom e-consumers are protected in the online market and what issues need to be addressed in order to protect them. The next section discusses the basic rights of consumers and the justification for e-consumer protection.

E-Consumer Rights and E-Consumer Protection

Similar to traditional commerce, there have been some forms of market failure in the online marketplace. For example, information asymmetry may occur due to insufficient information posted on commercial websites. Another example is bad business practices adopted by e-retailers which may cause market inefficiency and negative externality, that is, tarnish the reputation of the industry. WTO (2020) explained that:

> Online consumer protection is one of the challenges that the COVID-19 pandemic has highlighted. There have been reports of fraudulent and deceptive practices, with some online sellers

offering fake or unsafe hand sanitizers, surgical face masks or disinfectants for sale, and of price-gouging practices by certain manufacturers and retailers seeking to cash in and profit from the surge in demand. (p. 5)

E-consumer protection in e-retailing is defined as the protection of consumers' interests in commercial transactions by implementing regulation/guidelines, coregulation, and self-regulation (Ha 2017; Romanosky 2016; Subirana and Bain 2005). Such protection includes the policies and activities of government, e-retailers, and industry and consumer associations to address issues associated with e-retailing and to protect the consumer rights of citizens who shop online (Ha and McGregor 2013).

In 1962, to empower general consumers in social and economic activities, President John Kennedy of the United States introduced four basic consumer rights: the rights to (i) safety, (ii) information, (iii) choice, and (iv) representation (Consumers International 2006; Ha and Coghill 2008). These rights were adopted by various international consumer organizations. Later, another four rights were added as a result of the consumer movement led by Consumers International (USA) (Consumers International 2006). In 1985, the United Nations adopted the eight basic consumer rights, namely the rights to (i) safety, (ii) be informed, (iii) choose, (iv) be heard, (v) satisfaction of basic needs, (vi) redress, (vii) consumer education, and (viii) a healthy environment (Ha 2017; Ha and Coghill 2008; Singh 2002). However, these rights apply to consumers in both online and offline markets. They were not specially designed for e-consumers. The UN's guidelines were reviewed and revised in 1999, and then in 2015 in order to be up-to-date and can address the current and emerging issues and challenges encountered by consumers all over the world (Consumers International 2020).

Therefore, consumer protection aims to "protect the interest[s] of consumers" in commercial transactions (Quirk and Forder 2003, p. 300). Consumer protection is a channel to implement the eight universal basic consumer rights. Also, the development of e-retailing has entailed a number of e-consumer protection issues which have been "uniquely e-related" because some issues only occur on the online environment, such as phishing, spam, and computer viruses (Round and Tustin 2004b, p. 1).

This study focuses on e-consumer protection in e-retailing because of "lack of adequate [e-]consumer protection" (Goldsmith and McGregor 2000, p. 124) and lack of respect for consumer rights (Scottish Consumer Council 2001). E-consumers are entitled to enjoy the eight basic consumer rights and should be treated the same as consumers in traditional commerce. E-consumers must be protected from harmful products and services, and must be enabled to receive precise and relevant information to make an informed decision (World Economic Forum 2019). They have the right to select different products and services, and pay for these products and services at a competitive and fair price. They also have the right to receive products and services with acceptable quality. Additionally, e-consumers must be allowed to voice their concerns and to participate in the policy-making process (OECD 2016). Apart from having the right to enjoy basic essential goods and services, e-consumers must receive "a fair settlement of just claims, including compensation for misrepresentation, shoddy goods or unsatisfactory services" (NSW Office of Fair Trading undated, p. 1). However, e-consumers perceive that they have not been adequately protected even though they take more risks in e-transactions (Office of Communications (UK) 2006). For instance, they cannot inspect, touch, and feel goods before purchasing. Usually, they do not know who the e-retailers are, except from the well-known e-retailers, but they have to accept all terms and conditions in an e-contract without negotiation and have to pay in advance without any guarantee that goods will be delivered and delivered on time (Fletcher 2020; Greene 2020; Huffmann 2004; Petty and Hamilton 2004; Scottish Consumer Council 2001).

Furthermore, protecting e-consumers also means protecting e-retailers and the economy since "effective consumer protection is also essential to the functioning of the economy as a whole" (Pantelouri 2001, p. 2). When e-consumers' trust and confidence increase, their purchase intentions will increase and vice versa (Oliveira et al. 2017).

E-consumer protection has been the main focus in this volume because "consumption [was] the sole end and purpose of all production"

(Hilton 2005, p. 7). Although there have been many surveys gathering data about e-consumer behaviors in e-retailing, the Scottish Consumer Council (2001) highlights that nobody asks

> consumers how much protection they [felt] they [had] if something goes wrong with an online transaction. (p. 1)

Overall, e-consumer protection plays an essential role in building and maintaining trust and relationship between e-retailers and e-consumers (APEC Secretariat 2020).

Governance and E-Consumer Protection

Since e-consumers are directly affected by any legal consequences regarding e-consumer protection, not only consumer representatives but e-consumers must also be involved in the consultation process so that their concerns can be "better integrated" into relevant policies (Pantelouri 2001, p. 5). Therefore, exploration of the roles of e-consumers, e-retailers, and CSOs contributes to enhancing the democratic value in the process of governance of e-retailing. Also, the involvement in the governance process of different groups of stakeholders, especially e-consumers, facilitates the development of a "more inclusive style of policy making" process which can ensure good governance (Pantelouri 2001).

Vigoda (2002) concurred with Saward (1996) on the importance of responsiveness in governance. Responsiveness is reflected through political equality, the specification of "citizen democratic rights," and the design of mechanisms and institutions to achieve maximization of responsiveness (p. 470). Responsiveness reflects the connection between "citizens' preferences and government actions" (Soroka and Wlezien 2004, p. 531) and is also one of the principles of good governance (World Conference on Governance 1999). Responsiveness affects the capacity of consumers (people) and relevant government and CSOs (institutions) to interact effectively with each other which, in turn, affects "the capacity of a society, as a complex system," to adapt to changes in e-retailing (Coghill 2003, p. 11). As mentioned earlier, this implies that e-consumers, as citizens, must receive the same level of protection as other citizens no matter where they shop, that is, online or offline. They also have the right to be included in the governance of e-retailing. Therefore, governance for e-consumers has also been examined in chapters 3 and 4.

Conclusion

This chapter has defined the key concepts pertaining to e-retailing and e-consumer protection. It has explained the importance of e-consumer protection in e-retailing and the significance of this study regarding governance and e-consumer protection.

Although a mixture of measures has been implemented to protect e-consumers, the desired outcomes have not fully materialized. A standalone, extreme approach of governance, such as strict regulation or self-regulation, is inadequate to address the issues related to e-consumer protection. Either too much government intervention or lack of initiatives from business and lack of participation of civil society can hinder the development of e-retailing and discourage consumers from shopping online. A governance model which comprises all groups of stakeholders and can utilize the strengths of both the regulatory and self-regulatory approaches is worthy of research. Thus, this book will propose a four-sector governance model which may better explain the operation of e-consumer protection and could assist the development of more effective measures to protect e-consumers. The next chapter, Chapter 2, reviews the literature regarding the issues associated with e-consumer protection in the context of ASEAN countries.

References

Aïmeur, E., O. Lawani, and K. Dalkir. 2016. "When Changing the Look of Privacy policies Affects User Trust: An Experimental Study." *Computers in Human Behavior* 58, 368–379.

Alboukrek, K. 2003. "Adapting to a New World of E-Commerce: The Need for Uniform Consumer Protection in the International Electronic Marketplace." *The George Washington International Law Review* 35, no. 2, pp. 425–460.

APEC Secretariat. 2020. *Regulations, Policies and Initiatives on E-Commerce and Digital Economy for APEC MSMEs' Participation in the Region.* Singapore: APEC Secretariat.

Aragoncillo, L., and C. Orús. 2018. "Impulse buying behavior: An Online-Offline Comparative and the Social Media." *Spanish Journal of Marketing - ESIC* 22, no. 1, pp. 42–62.

Clement, J. 2020. *Factors Affecting U.S. Shopping Decisions During Coronavirus Pandemic April 2020. Statista,* 19 June 2020. https://statista.com/statistics/1121677/us-factors-affect-online-shopping-decisions-coronavirus/

Coghill, K. 2003. *Towards Governance for Uncertain Times: Joining up Public, Business and Civil Society Sectors.* CBR Working Paper no. 269. Cambridge: Judge School of Management, Cambridge University.

Consumer Affairs Victoria. 2003. *Victorian Consumers Face Problems Shopping Online.* Victoria: Consumer Affairs Victoria. http://dpc.vic.gov.au/domino/Web_Notes/newmedia.nsf/bc348d5912436a9cca256cfc0082d800/a45d2bb54b8bde3dca256ce6007acfcb!OpenDocument

Consumer Affairs Victoria. 2004. *Online Shopping and Consumer Protection: Discussion Paper* Melbourne, Victoria: Standing Committee of Officials of Consumer Affairs - E-commerce Working Party, Consumer Affairs Victoria.

Consumers International. 2006. *World Consumer Rights Day.* London: Consumers International. http://consumersinternational.org/Templates/Internal.asp?NodeID=95043&int1stParentNodeID=89651&int2ndParentNodeID=90145

Consumers International. 2020. *UN Guidelines for Consumer Protection.* London: Consumer Internationals.

Deloitte. 2015. *The Deloitte Consumer Review – Consumers under Attack: The Growing Threats of Cyber Crime.* UK: Deloitte LLP.

Dobbs, R., Y. Chen, G. Orr, J. Manyika, M. Chui, and E. Chang. 2013. *China's E-tail Revolution: Online Shopping as a Catalyst for Growth.* McKinsey Global Institute.

Doolin, B., Dillon, S., Thompson, F., and J. L. Corner. 2005. "Perceived Risk, the Internet Shopping Experience and Online Purchasing Behavior: A New Zealand Perspective." *Journal of Global Information Management* 13, pp. 2–26.

Duch-Brown, N., L. Grzybowski, A. Romahn, and F. Verboven. 2017. "The Impact of Online Sales on Consumers and firms. Evidence from consumer electronics." *International Journal of Industrial Organization,* 52, pp. 30–62.

Fergusson, M. 2000. "An Internet Business Framework for Government Agencies." In *Electronic Commerce: Opportunity and Challenges,* eds. S.M. Rahman, and M.S. Rasinghani. Hershey and London: Idea Group Publishing.

Goldsmith, E., and S.L.T. McGregor. 2000. "E-commerce: Consumer Protection No.s and Implications for Research and Education." *Consumer Studies & Home Economics* 24, no. 2, pp. 124–127.

Greene, J. 2020. "Frustrated Amazon Shoppers Vent at Record Levels." *The Washington Post,* May 21, 2020. https://washingtonpost.com/technology/2020/05/21/amazon-shopper-complaints/

Ha, H. 2012. "Online Security and Consumer Protection in E-commerce—An Australian Case." In *Strategic and Pragmatic E-Business: Implications for Future Business Practices* ed. K.M. Rezaul, 217–243. Hershey, PA: IGI Global.

Ha, H. 2013. "Credit Card Use and Risks in the E-Market: A Case Study in Melbourne, Australia." In eds. Hatem El-Gohary, and R. Eid. *E-Marketing in Developed and Developing Countries: Emerging Practices*, 214–232. USA: IGI Global.

Ha, H. 2017. "Stakeholders' Views on Self-Regulation to Protect Consumers in E-Retailing." *Journal of Electronic Commerce in Organizations* 15, no. 3, pp. 83–103.

Ha, H., and K. Coghill. 2008. "Online Shoppers in Australia: Dealing with Problems." *International Journal of Consumer Studies* 32, no. 1, pp. 5–17.

Ha, H., and S.L.T. McGregor. 2013. "Role of Consumer Associations in the Governance of E-commerce Consumer Protection." *Journal of Internet Commerce* 12, no. 1, pp. 1–25.

Hilton, M. 2005. "The Duties of Citizens, the Rights of Consumers." *Consumer Policy Review* 15, no. 1, pp. 6–12.

Huffmann, H. 2004. *Consumer Protection in E-Commerce*. Cape Town: Faculty of Law, School for Advanced Legal Studies, University of Cape Town.

Hui, T-K., and D. Wan. 2007. "Factors affecting Internet Shopping Behavior in Singapore: Gender and Educational Issues." *International Journal of Consumer Studies* 3, no. 1, pp. 310–316.

Invest Northern Ireland. undated. Grow Your Retail Business. Belfast: Invest Northern Ireland. https://nibusinessinfo.co.uk/content/advantages-and-disadvantages-online-retailing

Kaushik, V., A. Kumar, H. Gupta, and G. Dixit. 2020. "Modelling and Prioritizing the Factors for Online Apparel Return Using BWM Approach." Electronic Commerce Research (online). https://doi-org.ezproxy.newcastle.edu.au/10.1007/s10660-020-09406-3

Kim, J.H., and S. Lennon. 2012. "Electronic Retailing and Service Quality." In *Service Management: The New Paradigm in Retailing*. ed. J. Kandampully, 97–116. New York: Springer-Verlag.

Kita, P., Z. Szczyrba, D. Fiedor, and A. Letal. 2018. "Recognition of Business Risks When Purchasing Goods on the Internet using GIS: Experience from Slovakia." Electronic Commerce Research 18, pp. 647–663. https://doi-org.ezproxy.newcastle.edu.au/10.1007/s10660-017-9276-5

Lin, X., X. Wang, and N. Hajli. 2019. "Building E-Commerce Satisfaction and Boosting Sales: The Role of Social Commerce Trust and Its Antecedents." *International Journal of Electronic Commerce* 23, no. 3, pp. 328–363.

Lokken, S.L., G.W. Cross, L.K. Halbert, G. Lindsey, C. Derby, and C. Stanford. 2003. "Comparing Online and Non-online Shoppers." *International Journal of Consumer Studies* 27, no. 2, pp. 126–133.

Mann, M.K., and Y. Liu-Thompkins. 2019. "Shopping Online? The Role of Imagination and Gender." *European Journal of Marketing* 53, no. 12, pp. 2604–2628.

NSW Office of Fair Trading. undated. *International Consumer Rights: The World View on International Consumer Rights.* Parramatta: NSW Office of Fair Trading. https://fairtrading.nsw.gov.au/help-centre/youth-and-seniors/youth/international-consumer-rights

Oliveira, T., M. Alhinho, P. Rita, and G. Dhillon. 2017. "Modelling and Testing Consumer Trust Dimensions in E-commerce." *Computer Human Behavior* 71, pp. 153–164.

OECD. 2002. "Measuring the Information Economy 2002." *Science & Information Technology* 1, no. 76 14, pp. 190.

OECD. 2016. Consumer Protection in E-commerce OECD Recommendation. Paris: OECD.

Office of Communications (UK). 2006. *Online Protection: A Survey of Consumer, Industry and Regulatory Mechanisms and Systems.* London: Office of Communications (UK).

Pantelouri, A. 2001. "Speech by Pantelouri, A." *Conference on Consumer Policy, Market Economy and Democracy; Stockholm, 18–19 June 2001.* Stockholm: European Commission.

Petty, R.D., and J. Hamilton. 2004. "Seeking a Single Policy for Contractual Fairness to Consumers: A Comparison of U.S. and E.U Efforts." *Journal of Consumer Affairs* 38, no. 1, pp. 146–166.

Quirk, P., and J. Forder. 2003. *Electronic Commerce and The Law*, 2nd ed. Queensland: John Wiley & Sons Australia, Ltd.

Rahman, S.M. 2000. "Electronic Commerce at the Dawn of the Third Millennium." In *Electronic Commerce: Opportunity and Challenges*, eds. Rahman, S.M. and Raisinghani, M.S. Hershey and London: Idea Group Publishing.

Romanosky, S. 2016. "Examining the Costs and Causes of Cyber Incidents." *Journal of Cybersecurity* 2, no. 2, 121–135. https://doi.org/10.1093/cybsec/tyw001

Saward, M. 1996. "Democracy and Competing Values." *Government and Opposition* 31, no. 4, pp. 467–486.

Scottish Consumer Council. 2001. *E-Commerce and Consumer Protection: Consumers—Real Needs in a Virtual World.* Glasgow: Scottish Consumer Council.

Singh, B. 2002. *Consumer Education on Consumer Rights and Responsibilities, Code of Conduct for Ethical Business, Importance of Product Labelling.* Kuala Lumpur: Consumers International.

Soroka, S.N., and C. Wlezien. 2004. "Opinion Representation and Policy Feedback: Canada in Comparative Perspective." *Canadian Journal of Political Science* 37, no. 3, pp. 531–559.

Subirana, B., and M. Bain. 2005. "Consumer Protection." *Legal Programming: Designing Legally Compliant RFID and Software Agent Architectures for Retail Processes and Beyond.* US: Springer.

Vigoda, E. 2002. "From Responsiveness to Collaboration: Governance, Citizens, and the Next Generation of Public Administration." *Public Administration Review* 62, no. 5, pp. 527–540.

Wagner, G. H. Schramm-Klein, and S. Steinman. 2020. "Online Retailing Across E-channels and E-Channel Touchpoints: Empirical Studies of Consumer Behavior in the Multichannel E-Commerce Environment." *Journal of Business Research* 107, no. c, pp. 256–270.

Weill, P., and M.R. Vitale. 2001. *Place to Space - Migrating to eBusiness Models.* Boston, Massachusetts: Harvard Business School Press.

World Economic Forum. 2019. The Global Governance of Online Consumer Protection and E-commerce Building Trust. Cologny: World Economic Forum.

WTO. 2020. *E-Commerce, Trade and the Covid-19 Pandemic.* Geneva: WTO.

CHAPTER 2

Issues Associated With E-Consumer Protection

Introduction

It has been observed that "unfair, misleading and fraudulent commercial practices are on the rise" (OECD 2020, para. 5). This has been reflected in the 2017 survey conducted by the U.S. Federal Trade Commission (2019), which reported that the number of e-transaction frauds has steadily increased, and e-transaction frauds accounted for 54 percent of the total number of fraudulent incidents. The survey also found that female e-consumers and e-consumers aged 35 to 54 were more likely to be victims of fraud than others (U.S. Federal Trade Commission 2019). In the United States, the number of e-consumers' complaints about COVID-19 fraud reported from January 2020 to mid-April 2020 was 22,000, and the value of e-consumers' losses reached more than U.S.$22 million (OECD 2020). Cybercrime has steadily increased in Singapore, from 6,215 cases reported in 2018 to 9,430 cases in 2019 (Cyber Security Agency of Singapore (CSA) 2020). Importantly, these cases accounted for 26.8 percent of overall crimes in Singapore in 2019 (Cyber Security Agency of Singapore (CSA) 2020). In light of this, this chapter discusses the issues associated with e-consumer protection: information disclosure, product (including goods and services) quality, privacy, security, redress, and jurisdiction.

Although e-retailing was considered as another channel for commercial exchange and thus subject to the same rules and regulations as conventional transactions by the OECD (2000a), significant differences between e-retailing and traditional commerce have been observed by many authors, such as Chen and Dubinsky (2003), Ha (2017), Ha and Coghill (2008), Ha, Coghill and Maharaj (2009), Komiak and Benbasat (2004), and Weill and Vitale (2001). E-retailing provides nonphysical platforms for buyers and sellers (and also observers, reviewers, and the community) to interact and complete transactions online. Benefits of online transactions have been reported, including convenience, transactions being done at anytime from anywhere, more choices, better prices, and time saving to travel to physical shops (Ha 2011; 2013a; 2013b; 2017).

Nevertheless, information about businesses and products, prices, unsecured online payment methods, product delivery and quality, privacy, security, redress, inaccessible dispute mechanisms, and jurisdiction concerns also affect e-consumers' decisions on purchasing online (Tanodomdej 2017). Problems with e-retailing can be grouped into six main categories that are associated with e-consumer protection: (i) information disclosure, (ii) product quality, (iii) security, (iv) privacy, (v) redress, and (vi) jurisdiction (Australian Competition and Consumer Commission 2003; Calliess 2006; Ghosh 1998; Ha and Coghill 2008; OECD 2006a; 2006b). The six issues associated with e-consumer protection are derived from a literature review, from basic consumer rights, and from the concerns of various stakeholder groups. They are also identified from the factors that discourage e-consumers from shopping online, which were found by various studies (Ha 2011; 2012; 2013a; 2017; Ha, Coghill and Maharaj 2008; Ha and McGregor 2013; Ong 2005).

As summarized in Chapter 1, these six issues associated with e-consumer protection are the main focus in this chapter for the following reasons. First, the third basic consumer right endorsed by the United Nations (Consumers International 2006) stipulates that e-consumers have the right to receive clear, timely, and comprehensive information about products in order to make informed decisions and to select what products to buy, what brands to buy, and from which e-retailers to buy (Chan 2004; Dennis et al. 2004; Ha and Coghill 2008). Lack of relevant information prevents e-consumers from exercising their right, and insufficient and/or misleading information could lead to a dispute. On the contrary, adequate, timely, and precise information can improve e-consumer trust and confidence in e-retailers, which, in turn, can enhance the reputation of the industry (Chu, Choi and Song 2005; Ha and Coghill 2008; Ong 2005). Information and knowledge will make e-consumers feel more empowered (Pires, Stanton and Rita 2006). E-consumers who are more knowledgeable about products, processes, and e-retailing have more control over their online purchases, and thus they would have stronger intentions to purchase online (Dyke et al. 2007; Milloy et al. 2002). In addition, the second consumer right—right to safety (safety has a wide coverage, e.g., product safety, personal safety)—indicates that e-consumers should receive that product whose quality is acceptable and is safe to use (Ha 2012; 2013; 2017).

Second, the development of e-retailing also brings about several issues of data privacy and online security that are the main inhibitors to e-retailing (Ha 2011; Milloy et al. 2002). These two concerns are closely related and must be inspected together since the lack of online security measures may lead to the disclosure of e-customers' private and confidential information. Since e-consumers have the right to safety according to the second consumer right, they must be protected against existing and potential privacy and security risks associated with e-retailing. In addition, many e-consumers are not aware that the amount of work, time, and effort involved in "restoring [their] credit record [or clearing their names]" is exhausting (*The Age* 2007, p. 1). Thus, there is strong evidence for the inclusion of these issues when examining e-consumer protection.

Finally, e-consumers are entitled to seek redress as stated in the sixth consumer right. Redress enables e-consumers to enjoy their basic rights and increases the efficacy of the marketplace (Hogarth and English 2002). Redress in e-retailing is intertwined with jurisdiction. Legal ambiguity creates difficulties and complications of claims when e-consumers want to seek redress, especially when it is not clear which court in which jurisdiction is responsible for making a decision on a particular case (Ha 2008; Subirana and Bain 2005). Additionally, the degree of trust changes when e-consumers shift from traditional commerce to e-retailing (Komiak and Benbasat 2004). Overall, the classification of these issues is consistent with the key issues discussed by Ha (2008), Ha, Coghill and Maharaj (2008), the OECD (2000a), and Subirana and Bain (2005) that emphasized the disclosure of relevant information on websites, the determination of jurisdiction in legal procedures and implications for e-transactions, complaint handling and redress, the provision of secure electronic payment systems, and the protection of data privacy. Overall, these issues are the pull factors that discourage e-consumers to shop online. They are very important in e-retailing given its cross-border nature, and the rapid speed and the immediate results of an e-transaction, and also because the e-transactions between sellers and buyers may happen at different time and in different locations (Attorney-General's Department (Australia) 2003; Ha and McGregor 2013; Komiak and Benbasat 2004).

E-Consumer Protection and the Six Associated Issues

The following section discusses the issues associated with e-retailing in detail.

Information Disclosure

When conducting online transactions, e-customers must provide their personal and financial information to e-retailers and agree to what is required by the e-retailers before they can proceed to the next step, that is, checking out from the cart, confirming the purchase, and making payment. E-consumers usually have to agree with all terms and conditions set by e-retailers without any opportunities for negotiation and have to make payment in advance if they want to proceed with the e-transactions (Ha 2012; 2013a; 2013b). In addition, e-customers do not know much about e-retailers, except the information provided on their websites which usually is easily modified, uploaded, or downloaded (Ha 2017; Scott 2004). It is also very difficult for e-consumers to assess the accuracy of information uploaded on e-retailers' websites (Scott 2004). Thus, some e-consumers rely on e-retailers' reputation, the available information on their websites, and the reviews by buyers who had purchased products of particular e-retailers.

Although information alone cannot ensure safety to e-consumers, information enables e-consumers to know the features of a product and the choice to buy or not to buy and be more aware of what they want when making their decision to purchase such a product online (Kierkegaard and Kierkegaard 2005). In other words, information facilitates an informed decision-making process. Any misleading or inaccurate information will affect the ability of e-customers to make an informed decision and will not be in their best interest (Department of Enterprise, Trade and Employment (UK) 2004; Scott 2004). In some cases, misleading or false information about medical products can endanger e-consumers' health and lives (Seçkin et al. 2016).

Added to this, sufficient and timely information enables e-retailers to build trust with e-customers (Pratima and Heggde 2018). The value of the information regarding prices in the online market can also be computed. Baye, Morgan, and Scholten (2003) calculate that e-consumers may have to pay between 11 percent and 20 percent more if they do not have sufficient access to information. Thus, three sets of information should be disclosed to e-consumers in a comprehensive and accurate manner (OECD 2016).

The first information set is about products and services. Due to the nature of the online market, e-consumers cannot check and inspect a product or try a service before purchasing it. As a result, they rely heavily on the information describing the products and services on e-retailers' websites. In this digital era, data-driven decision making (DDDM) would produce significant benefits to users, such as providing a benchmark for comparison, allowing proactive action, and saving costs (Harvard Business School 2019). Although price is considered as one of the most common factors encouraging e-consumers to make a purchase decision, "having a website that consumers like and/or trust is also important, especially in Asia, where consumers said buying from a preferred website was more important than price" (KPMG International Cooperative 2017, p. 20).

The second information set is about e-retailers and their businesses. E-customers need to know the identity/business name or trade mark, the registration status, and the location or jurisdiction where e-retailers register and operate their businesses (Scott 2004). Given geographical distances, e-consumers cannot visit e-retailers' outlets physically or contact e-retailers face-to-face, but they feel safer and more confident when dealing with e-retailers who they know or are recommended (Ha and Coghill 2008; Kierkegaard and Kierkegaard 2005). E-consumers also have the right to know who to contact and how to contact e-retailers when there are problems with the e-transactions (NSW Office of Fair Trading undated).

The third information set that needs to be disclosed to e-consumers concerns the transaction processes. Usually, e-consumers have to accept the terms and conditions stipulated by e-retailers on their websites before e-consumers can proceed to the next step. E-customers usually do not have an opportunity to discuss the sales agreement with e-retailers, but they have to make payment for the purchase(s) in advance. Thus, they should be provided with adequate information about sales terms and conditions, including prices, discount, currency, payment process, delivery arrangements, warranties, returns, and refund/exchange, especially the cooling-off period, to see whether they can commit to such conditions (Consumer Affairs Victoria 2004; Hockey 1999, 2000; OECD 2002b). Nondisclosure of information regarding terms and conditions, as well as redress and dispute resolution would deter e-consumers from obtaining fair treatment in business transactions. Relevant information is needed to empower e-consumers to seek compensation when problems with e-transactions arise (Dyke et al. 2007; Ha 2017; Ha and McGregor 2013; Harrison, Waite and Hunter 2006). As a result, e-retailers who fail to disclose necessary information are considered "breaching" fair trading practices (Kierkegaard and Kierkegaard 2005).

Furthermore, relevant information should be timely and effectively communicated to e-consumers, and the language should be clear in order to convey the content to e-consumers in a simple and precise manner, that is, an ordinary person without any legal background can understand it. Overflow of information or insufficient information on the online market makes it very difficult for e-customers to filter the necessary information that can help them improve the quality of their purchase decisions (Glenn and Gordon 2005). Lastly, e-consumers must be entitled to have access to any records related to e-purchases for any postsales services and posttransaction communication (OECD 2002b). According to KPMG International Cooperative (2017), millennials form the biggest e-consumers and they also need information provided in a way that is both entertaining and informative. However, many e-retailers do not provide sufficient information about products/services, terms and conditions, and their businesses on their websites (Consumer Affairs Victoria 2004; Hockey 1999; Mayer 2002). Thus, information disclosure should be considered as one of the main factors affecting e-consumer protection.

Product Quality

Many countries have implemented consumer protection regulations in terms of safety standards of general consumer goods in traditional commerce (Australian Competition and Consumer Commission (ACCC) 2014; Enterprise Singapore 2018; U.S. Consumer Product Safety Commission 2019; business.gov.au 2020). Thus, this should also apply to e-consumers although it is advised that e-consumers should exercise caution and take ownership of their own safety, that is, the principle of *caveat emptor* exists (Enterprise Singapore 2018). E-consumers should exercise the same level of precaution, either in the online or in the offline market even if it is more difficult for them to do so in the online market. Generally, consumers can do so by purchasing "goods from reliable and trustworthy suppliers, read and understand the labels, warnings and instructions that accompany the product and use the product only for the intended purpose" (Enterprise Singapore 2018, p. 5).

Security

Most e-users consider privacy and security as very critical in the online platforms (Ha 2008; 2017; Milloy et al. 2002; Miyazaki and Fernandez 2001). Although there are many security issues, this chapter focuses on the main issues, discussed by Ha (2012; 2013; 2017), given their relevance to e-consumer protection, namely, data security, payment security, phishing/pharming, and scams.

First, Ha (2011; 2012) explains that the safeguard of personal identify and financial information during various stages of an e-transaction, such as collection, transmission, and retention, is referred to as data security. There have been many cases of online identity theft which occurs when an e-consumer's personal identity is unlawfully acquired by various means and disseminated with the intention to commit a crime using electronic means (Ha 2012; 2013; Metz 2005).[1] For example, e-consumers' confidential information can be illegally acquired during the process

---

[1] Identity theft can also be considered a subissue of privacy.

of purchasing products online via e-retailers' websites. Possible violators can be internal stakeholders of an e-retailing, such as employees and managers, or outsiders, such as cyber hackers (Ha 2013a; 2013b; 2017).[2] A recent survey in the United States by SurveyMonkey reported that about one-quarter (22 percent) of the respondents reused the same password many times, and one-third (34 percent) of the respondents shared passwords or accounts with their colleagues (Williams 2019), that is, about "30 million of the 95 million American knowledge workers may be sharing passwords" (Williams 2019, para. 2). Personal and financial information can also be obtained, without the knowledge of the owners and/or even e-retailers, during the storing stage, especially when storage is easily accessed via electronic means (Milloy et al. 2002). Other methods to obtain information online are the use of computer viruses/worms, spyware, phreaking, smurfing and account harvesting, and many other forms of online risk. E-consumers do have concerns about security when they are online. The 2020 Unisys Security Index indicates that 41 percent of global consumers have concerns about data breach (Unisys 2020). The 2018 Unisys Security Index revealed that identity theft, bank card fraud, and Internet hacking and virus are the top three security issues for Malaysians (Unisys 2018). Thus, the concerns create barrier to consumers embracing "digital identity-based services" and one in three Malaysians would not deal with an organization after suffering a data breach (Unisys 2018, para. 1). The survey in the Philippines in 2019 revealed that 90 percent of respondents were worried about illegal access or misuse of their personal data, and 80 percent worried about credit card theft (Unisys 2019a, b).

Second, e-consumers are also worried about payment security because the misuse and theft of credit card details has increased over time when advanced technology may be misused to obtain e-consumers' financial information in a wrongful manner (OECD 2002c; Perumal and Shanmugam 2004). It was noted that the number of incidents pertaining to online card fraud was about 3 to 30 times higher than the amount of card fraud in traditional commerce (Centeno 2002). There is no doubt that payment by

---

[2] Examples of possible intruders are employees, independent hackers, criminal individuals, organized crime rings, business competitors, saboteurs, and cyber terrorists.

credit cards is one of the most popular online payment methods. Yet, monetary collection, saving, and transaction via online platforms do entail some security issues; the same goes to other cashless payment modes (Ha and Lin 2018). Consequently, if e-retailers do not have a proper payment system, e-consumers may receive less protection for e-payment (Ha 2011; 2017).

Ha (2012; 2013) explains that there are two subissues in payment security. The first issue relates to credit card detail disclosure, including credit card holders' names, credit card number, security code (CSV), and expiry date. Charge back or getting a refund is the second subissue in payment security (Ha 2012). Given the nature of online purchases, that is, the lack of opportunity to check physical products before purchasing them, many e-consumers have concerns if they can get a refund (when they decide that such products are not suitable to them in a later date), or an exchange for defective products or nondelivered products, and how to obtain the amount of money that is wrongly charged by e-retailers (Ha 2012).

The next issue is phishing and pharming. Phishing and pharming have been detected as the most popular and sophisticated methods to obtain personal and financial information online (Metz 2005; OECD 2006b). Purkait (2012) explained that "phishing is also known as the bait and hook method," that is, the phishers would use a bait, such as an e-mail or a phishing/fake website (usually a replica or an imitation of the website of a financial institution), to collect sensitive information of the e-users (p. 382). When e-users/victims provide their information online, such information is directed to the phishers who, then, will make use of them for their own personal interest (Purkait 2012). Pharming is another form of phishing for personal and financial information illegally. Swinhoe (2020) explained that a pharming attack would redirect the traffic of a website of an organization to a fake website that is managed by cyber attackers, who will obtain the victims' information illegally or install malware on their computers in order to harvest private and confidential data. This situation has become more serious since new forms of phishing, such as phishing-based Trojan keyloggers and redirectors, smishing (a subset of phishing, including phishing via SMS), and vishing (a subset of phishing, including phishing via voice), have been adopted by cyber criminals to commit a crime (Anti-Phishing Working Group 2006a; Glabbeed 2018; Musuva, Getao and Chepken 2019; Fruhlinger 2020). According to the

Anti-Phishing Working Group (2020), the number of phishing sites detected has increased from 162,155 in 2019 to 165,772 in 2020. The Cyber Security Agency of Singapore (CSA) (2019) reported that 47,500 Singapore-hosted phishing URLs were detected in 2019, a sharp increase from 16,100 URLs in 2018. There were 35 cases of ransomware reported by SingCERT (Singapore Computer Emergency Response Team) in 2019 (Cyber Security Agency of Singapore (CSA) (2020). According to the Interpol Global Complex for Innovation (2020), "Southeast Asia remains a target for cybercriminals attempting to infect networks and devices through the simple but effective trick of phishing" (p. 7). However, it should be noted that the number of undetected phishing sites is unknown.

Another issue associated with online security is scams. The most popular scam incidents have been the online dating scams (Norris, Brookes and Dowell 2019). Other popular forms of online scams include advance fee fraud, lottery and competition scams, employment scams, bargain prices, miracle products, high-profit investment, fake charity scams, and dubious business proposals (Northern Territory Government of Australia 2019; OECD 2020). Recently, scammers have exploited e-consumers' fear and anxiety of COVID-19 to promote fake products that can prevent or treat COVID-19 (OECD 2020). In Singapore, online scams are the most popular scam type, and the number of online scams increased from 2,161 cases in 2018, to 2,809 cases in 2019, that is, an increase of 30 percent (Cyber Security Agency of Singapore (CSA) 2020).

Overall, e-consumers have many concerns pertaining to online security, including credit card misuse and fraud. Added to this, online payment is "further complicated as payment systems may be subject to different regulatory schemes, which may have important implications with respect to the level of consumer protection afforded" (OECD 2014, p. 4). E-consumers are also worried about other technical threats, such as computer viruses, malware, ransomware, and computer worms. All these act to dampen e-consumers' intention to purchase online.

Privacy

Another important issue affecting e-consumers, when they shop online, is privacy (Stoney and Stoney 2003). Privacy issues and security issues are interrelated. As mentioned previously, e-consumers are very troubled about the collection, usage, and disclosure of personal data as well as their medical history (Ha 2017; Jackson 2003; Kehoe et al. 1999; Moghe 2003). Many e-consumers do not want to reveal their personal and financial information for fear of being misused. Yet, by adopting advanced technology, e-retailers can easily collect personal and financial details of e-consumers (Lynch 1997). Many e-retailers ask e-consumers to "register or accept" cookies which can help them in tracking the latter's Internet itinerary (Yianakos 2002, p. 48). As predicted by Pace (2020), privacy of consumers would continue taking priority in 2020 and beyond. However, even though privacy policies are posted on the websites, many of them are not comprehensive and are difficult to understand, that is, "exceed the college reading level" as noted by Litman-Navarro (2019, p. 6), and companies can actually collect and share customers' personal data even if they have privacy policy (Schlesinger and Day 2019).

There are three subissues of privacy: spam, spim (spam-over-instant-messaging), and spyware. Spam is considered as a subset of online privacy because spam can only occur if individuals' e-mail addresses are revealed and used without the owners' consent. Traditionally, spam is usually referred to as unsolicited/unwanted commercial e-mails (Federal Trade Commission 2011). Ferrara (2019) broadly defines spam as "the attempt to abuse of, or manipulate, a techno-social system by producing and injecting unsolicited, and/or undesired content" for the interest of spammer(s) (p. 3). The types of spam include e-mails, instant or mobile messages, search engines, social bots, etc. (Ferrara 2019). In many cases, e-consumers' personal e-mail addresses are stolen online or are shared with other parties by e-retailers or even by authorized persons in their companies (Ha 2012). Clement (2020) reported that about 53.95 percent of e-mail traffic in March 2020 is spam messages, and a lot of them are malicious, transmitting spyware, ransomware, and Trojans. More than one-third of the world's spam content is advertising messages, and more than a quarter of them are related to financial issues (Budanović 2019). Spam e-mails, targeting academics, cost higher education institutes about $1.1 billion every year (Baker 2020).

Apart from promoting unsolicited content that may relate to scams, deception, and unwanted advertisements of financial products, romance and love, bogus degrees, and fake news, a huge number of spam e-mails also take up a lot of valuable network resources of corporations and countries, especially those with limited Internet bandwidth (Internet

Society 2020). The cost of receiving unwanted spam messages via phones can be substantial. Also, the costs spent on repairing the systems that are attacked by "spam-enabled malware" and the costs spent on rectifying data breach are significant (Internet Society 2020). For example, the average cost of an online security breach for companies in Singapore is about S$1.7 million (around U.S.$1.25 million) per breach, about S$785,000 (around U.S.$577,200) in Indonesia, and about S$31,000 (around U.S.$22,795) in Malaysia (Henderson 2020).

Different from spams that are sent to receivers via conventional methods, spim is mainly produced by worms and other undesirable or sometimes illegal software (Osterman 2004). Such unwanted software has the ability to infect a machine, and people on the contact list of the machine owners become "spimmers without their knowledge or consent" (Osterman 2004). In fact, several years ago, the Australian Institute of Criminology (2006) and Ha (2012; 2013; 2017) warned Internet users about spim, a new form of spam, that often aims at instant messaging services. Table 2.1 summarizes key cyberattacks in Southeast Asian countries from 2018 to 2019. In these cases, the number of users affected by the incidents was huge.

Table 2.1 Key cyber incidents in ASEAN region (2018 to 2019)

Time line	Country	Incidents
March 2018	Thailand	Personal information of 45,000 customers of True Corp was disclosed
July 2018	Singapore	The records of 1.5 million patients of SingHealth were hacked and stolen
January 2019	Philippines	Personal information of 900,000 customers of Philippines Cebuana was revealed by a marketing server breach
March 2019	Thailand and Vietnam	The servers of Toyota Motor Corporation's subsidiaries in these countries were accessed illegally
September 2019	Southeast Asia	About 14 million phishing attempts to obtain e-users' sensitive information were found in the first two quarters of the year in the region

Source: Adapted from Interpol Global Complex for Innovation (2020).

The third subissue of privacy is spyware. Spyware is a form of malicious surveillance software that is installed on e-users' computers without their knowledge (Baharudin 2019; Molnar and Harkin 2019). Such spyware allows hackers to monitor e-users' behavior and steal sensitive information (Baharudin 2019). Spyware can also modify the browser settings of e-users or home pages of a website that may direct the e-users to fake or malicious sites (Majoras et al. 2005). Several computer and mobile malware attacks have been found in Southeast Asian countries (Ismail 2020). Yet, many e-users may not know about spyware (Internet Society 2017). In a survey of 2,000 people from 40 countries in Asia-Pacific region by the Internet Society (2017), 70 percent of participants did not think that their personal information was adequately protected online; and nearly 60 percent of them might not have adequate "knowledge and [right] tools to protect their privacy online" (para. 5). Thus, it is important to increase e-consumers' awareness of how to protect their privacy online and also to handle online privacy incidents (Ha 2012; 2017).

Overall, UNCTACD (2016) asserted that data protection is directly interrelated to the development of trade in products, especially in the digital economy. Also, "Insufficient protection can create negative market effects by reducing consumer confidence, and overly stringent protection can unduly restrict businesses, with adverse economic effects as a result" (UNCTACD 2016, p. x1). Yet, over- or underregulation will result in drawbacks and affect many stakeholders. Thus, the urgent task for all groups of stakeholders is to search for novel motivators and inducements to address the challenges associated with privacy protection that is made more complicated by the digital world (Ha 2012; Yianakos 2002). According to the first basic consumer right, e-consumers should be able to enjoy their right to be safe in terms of privacy. Hence, e-retailers should protect e-customers' privacy to the best of their ability because they are, by law, not allowed to disclose their customers' personal information without their knowledge and prior consent.

Redress

Redress in e-retailing is referred to the internal complaint-handling procedures by e-retailers that enables e-consumers to seek remedies or claim damages or address problems, occurring during e-transactions (Ong and The 2016). In e-retailing, problems pertaining to redress include the value of products purchased online, lack of internal complaint-handling policy, lack of information about available mechanisms to handle complaints, lack of alternative channels for dispute resolution, inaccessible dispute resolution, and lack of e-consumers' awareness of e-retailers' internal redress mechanisms (Ha 2017; Ha et al. 2009; OECD 2016; *Tanodomdej 2017*). In many cases, e-retailers' complaint-handling process is too time-consuming and complicated that deter e-consumers to pursue complaints. In addition, jurisdiction also poses challenges to both e-consumers and e-retailers when cross-jurisdiction disputes arise.

First, the features (e.g., size, content) and the monetary value of products purchased online do have an effect on e-consumers' decisions to lodge complaints to e-retailers when there are issues with such purchases (Cho et al. 2002). If the monetary value of a product purchased online is too small, e-consumers may find it too trivial and troublesome to ask for a refund or an exchange when the product purchased is defective or its quality is not acceptable (Ha et al. 2008). E-consumers are worried that the time and costs spent on refunding or exchanging products that are purchased online may even be higher than the amount of compensation (Ha and Coghill 2008).

Second, information about internal complaint-handling mechanisms is not sufficient or not available to e-consumers until issues arise. In many cases, e-consumers may not be aware of the redress policy of e-retailers. In many cases, e-consumers may not be able to contact e-retailers after payment is made (Ha et al. 2009; Yuthayotin 2014). Since e-consumers have "the right to access dispute resolution and to obtain redress" (UNCTAD 2018, p.2), insufficient information and/or nondisclosure of information regarding redress deters e-consumers from making informed decisions on seeking dispute resolution. The OECD (2017a) observed that uncertainties about redress mechanisms discourage e-consumers to shop online and thus slow down e-retailing growth.

Third, the World Economic Forum (2019) proposed that e-retailers and e-consumers should know about what rules and regulations are relevant and how to come to a solution when there are cross-national disputes during and after an e-transaction. However, e-consumers believe that the process of seeking redress in cross-border e-transactions is very complex, time-consuming, and onerous. As a result, many e-consumers do not pursue dispute cases involved in overseas e-retailers because of the complication of multijurisdictional litigation. They also feel that the costs, time, and effort spent on such cases may not be worthy, especially for relatively small values of purchases (Calliess 2006). Even if there are online dispute resolution (ORD) mechanisms, e-consumers may not have sufficient resources (time, information) and incentive to search for suitable ODR alternatives (Liyanage 2012).

In general, the OECD (2018a) asserted that e-consumers' right to redress should be respected, and they should be able to gain access to fair and easy-to-use redress mechanisms in order to resolve disputes without unjustified cost and inconvenience. However, Ong and The (2016) explained that e-consumers usually request for a speedy and effective redress procedure from e-retailers. However, litigation in traditional commerce to seek redress is not practical and not preferred by e-consumers or e-retailers. Thus, UNCTAD (2017) suggested that alternative dispute resolution mechanisms should be developed to offer e-consumers with effective and efficient solutions to address disputes between e-consumers and e-retailers who reside in different jurisdictions. Yet, e-consumers still have concerns about redress in e-transactions for many reasons. This suggests that there may be problems with enforcement and effectiveness of dispute resolutions mechanisms for e-transactions (Jawahitha 2005).

Jurisdiction

Ha (2017) and Ha et al. (2009) explained that there are three main issues pertaining to jurisdiction in e-retailing when there are disputes and e-consumers and e-retailers are in different jurisdictions. These issues are as follows: (i) What jurisdiction is applicable to a particular e-transaction when e-consumers and e-retailers are in different jurisdictions? (ii) Which law or regulations in the respective jurisdiction should be applied to the particular e-transaction between e-consumers and e-retailers? (iii) Which government authority(ies) will enforce the verdict and will be responsible for solving any subsequent dispute (Bygrave and Svantesson 2001; Hockey 1999)? The fact is that many e-consumers may not know the physical location of e-retailers with whom they are transacting and where their businesses are registered (Scott 2004). Actually, it is more difficult for e-consumers to address cyber incidents because of different governance

and regulatory frameworks of e-consumer protection from different jurisdictions (Ha 2011; UNCTAD 2017).

Ward, Sipior and Volonino (2016) asserted that the cross-border
nature of e-retailing does entail issues of Internet jurisdiction (or cyber
jurisdiction). These authors explained that e-consumers and e-retailers do
face legal risk in e-transactions. Some examples of legal actions pertaining
to e-retailing include "computer crime, contracts, copyright, defamation
and libel, discrimination, fraud, hacking, harassment, intellectual prop-
erty, obscenity and pornography, privacy, taxation, trade secrets, and trade-
mark" (Ward et al. 2016, p. 3). Jurisdiction in cross-border e-transactions
is vague, and both e-consumers and e-retailers do want to be involved in
distant jurisdictions when disputes arise (Ong 2005; Ward et al. 2016).

Overall, advanced technology enables e-retailers to easily move virtually
from one jurisdiction to another, and it is problematic to enforce a local
verdict against an overseas e-retailer (Jawahitha 2005). This does not mean
that e-consumers may not encounter any problems when they purchase
from e-retailers in the same jurisdiction. However, in many cases, it is more
costly to settle disputes with e-retailers in different jurisdictions because
the expense spent to pursue litigation cases in the plaintiff's (e-consumers')
home country is about 3 percent lower than if the cases are brought up in
the defendant's country (e-retailers') (Patel and Lindley 2001).

Conclusion

This chapter discussed the six issues associated with e-consumers, namely
(i) information disclosure, (ii) product quality, (iii) security, (iv) privacy,
(v) redress, and (vi) jurisdiction. The association of these six issues with
e-consumer protection has been justified. The six issues associated with
e-consumer protection are caused by a combination of legality, finance,
technology, and human behavior, which require simultaneous actions by
different groups of stakeholders to address them effectively. These issues
are interconnected and should be addressed simultaneously. Thus, it
requires strong cooperation among stakeholders, in either the same or
different jurisdictions, to effectively address these issues. Without such
cooperation, efforts of individuals or individual organizations may be
futile, and a zero sum game is inevitable.

The next chapter will discuss concepts and theories of e-consumer protection governance, including the role of the three sectors relevant to e-consumer protection, namely (i) the state, (ii) the private sector, and (iii) civil society organizations.

References

Anti-Phishing Working Group. 2020. *Phishing Activity Trends Report: 1st quarter 2020*. Anti-Phishing Working Group.

Attorney-General's Department (Australia). 2003. *Inquiry into Cybercrime*. Barton, ACT: Attorney-General's Department (Australia).

Australian Competition and Consumer Commission. 2003. *Review of Building Consumer Sovereignty in Electronic Commerce (Best Practice Model)*. Treasury (Australia).

Australian Competition and Consumer Commission. 2014. *Consumer Product Safety Online*. Canberra: Commonwealth of Australia.

Baharudin, H. 2019. "What is Spyware and How does it Affect Organizations and Individuals?" *The Straits Times*, 20 May 2019.

Baker, S. 2020. "Dealing with spam emails 'costs academia more than peer review." *Times Higher Education*, January 9, 2020. https://timeshighereducation.com/news/dealing-spam-emails-costs-academia-more-peer-review

Budanović, N. 2019. "20 Spam Statistics that Shed Light on the Dark Side of Your Inbox." *DataProt*, December 11, 2019. https://dataprot.net/statistics/spam-statistics/

business.gov.au. 2020. *Product Safety Rules and Standards*. Canberra: Commonwealth of Australia. https://business.gov.au/Products-and-services/Product-labelling/Product-safe ty-rules-and-standards

Bygrave, L.A., and D. Svantesson. 2001. "Jurisdictional Issues and Consumer Protection in Cyberspace: The View from Down Under." *Cyberspace Law Resource* 12, pp. 1–12.

Calliess, G.P. 2006. "Online Dispute Resolution: Consumer Redress in a Global Market Place." *German Law Journal* 7, no. 8, pp. 647–660.

Centeno, C. 2002. *Building Security and Consumer Trust in Internet Payments: The Potential of "Soft" Measure*. Seville, Spain: Institute for Prospective Technological Studies.

Chan, P. 2004. "Measuring the Effectiveness of Consumer Protection." *Consumer Policy Review* 14, pp. 1–22.

Chen, Z., and A.J. Dubinsky. 2003. "A Conceptual Model of Perceived Customer Value in E-Commerce: A Preliminary Investigation." *Psychology & Marketing* 20, no. 4, pp. 323–347.

Cho, Y., I. Im, R. Hiltz, and J. Fjermestad. 2002. "An Analysis of Online Customer Complaints: Implications for Web Complaint Management." Paper read at the 35th Hawaii International Conference on System Science, Hawaii.

Chu, W., B. Choi, and M.R. Song. 2005. "The Role of On-line Retailer Brand and Infomediary Reputation in Increasing Consumer Purchase Intention." *International Journal of Electronic Commerce* 9, no. 3, pp. 115–127.

Clement, J. 2020. "Spam: share of global email traffic 2014-2020." *Statista*, June 24, 2020. https://statista.com/statistics/420391/spam-email-traffic-share/

Consumer Affairs Victoria. 2004. *Online Shopping and Consumer Protection: Discussion Paper.* Melbourne, Victoria: Standing Committee of Officials of Consumer Affairs - E-commerce Working Party, Consumer Affairs Victoria.

Consumers International. 2006. *World Consumer Rights Day.* London: Consumers International. http://consumersinternational.org/Templates/Internal.asp?NodeID=95043&int1stParentNodeID =89651&int2ndParentNodeID= 90145

Cyber Security Agency of Singapore (CSA). 2020. *Singapore Cyber Landscape 2019.* Singapore: Cyber Security Agency of Singapore. https://csa.gov.sg/news/publications/singapore-cyber-landscape-2019

Dennis, C., T. Fenech, and B. Merrilees. 2004. *e-Retailing.* London and New York, NY: Routledge, Taylor & Francis Group.

Dyke, T.P.V., V. Midha, and H. Nemati. 2007. "The Effect of Consumer Privacy Empowerment on Trust and Privacy Concerns in E-Commerce." *Electronic Markets* 17, no. 1, pp. 68–81.

Enterprise Singapore. 2018. *Consumer Protection (Consumer Goods Safety Requirements) Regulations 2011 (CGSR).* Information Booklet (Edition 5). Singapore: Enterprise Singapore.

Federal Trade Commission. 2011. *Spam.* USA: Federal Trade Commission.

Ferrara, E. 2019. "The History of Digital Spam." *Communications of the ACM* 62, no. 8, pp. 82–91.

Fruhlinger, J. 2020. "Vishing Explained: How Voice Phishing Attacks Scam Victims." *CSO*, May 18, 2020. https://csoonline.com/article/3543771/vishing-explained-how-voice-phishing-attacks-scam -victims.html

Ghosh, A.K. 1998. *E-commerce Security: Weak Links, Best Defenses.* New York, NY: John Wiley & Sons, Inc.

Glabbeed, J.V. 2019. "'Smishing': The New SMS Fraud." *TechRadar*, December 17, 2019. https://techradar.com/sg/news/smishing-the-new-sms-fraud

Ha, H. 2011. "Security and Privacy in E-consumer Protection in Victoria, Australia." 5th International Conference on Trust Management (TM), June 2011, Copenhagen, Denmark. pp. 240–252.

Ha, H. 2012. "Online Security and Consumer Protection in Ecommerce-An Australian Case." In *Strategic and Pragmatic E-Business: Implications for Future Business Practices*, ed. K.M. Rezaul, 217–243. Hershey, PA: IGI Global.

Ha, H. 2013a. "Credit Card Use and Risks in the E-Market: A Case Study in Melbourne, Australia." In *E-Marketing in Developed and Developing Countries: Emerging Practices,* eds. H. El-Gohary, and R. Eid, 214232. USA: IGI Global.

Ha, H. 2013b. "Credit Card Use and Debt by Female Students - A Case Study in Melbourne, Australia." *Youth Studies Australia* 32, no. 4., Online.

Ha, H. 2017. "Stakeholders' Views on Self-Regulation to Protect Consumers in E-Retailing." *Journal of Electronic Commerce in Organizations* 15, no. 3, pp. 83–103.

Ha, H., and K. Coghill. 2008. "Online Shoppers in Australia: Dealing with Problems." *International Journal of Consumer Studies* 32, no. 1, pp. 5–17.

Ha, H., K. Coghill, and E.A. Maharaj. 2009. "Current Measures to Protect E-consumers' Privacy in Australia." In *Online Consumer Protection: Theories of Human Relativism,* eds. K. Chen, and A. Fadlalla, 123150. Hershey, PA: Idea Group, Inc.

Ha, H., and C. Lin. 2018. "Commentary: Hawkers want to Embrace Cashless Payments but Say they Need Help Tackling Barriers." *Channel News Asia,* December 19, 2018. https://channelnewsasia.com/news/commentary/hawkers-cashless-payments-need-help-barrie rs-to-adoption-11042450

Ha, H., and S.L.T. McGregor. 2013. "Role of Consumer Associations in the Governance of E-commerce Consumer Protection." *Journal of Internet Commerce* 12, no. 1, pp. 1–25.

Harrison, T., L. Waite, and G.L. Hunter. 2006. "The Internet, Information and Empowerment." *European Journal of Marketing* 40, nos. 9/10, pp. 972–993.

Harvard Business School. 2019. *The Advantages of Data-Driven Decision-Making.* Harvard Business School (online), August 29, 2019. https://online.hbs.edu/blog/post/data-driven-decision-making

Henderson, J. 2020. "Security Attacks Cost Singaporean Businesses $1.7M per breach." *Channel News Asia,* January 21, 2020. https://sg.channelasia.tech/article/670400/ security-attacks-cost-singaporean-businesses-1-7m-per-breach/

Hockey, J. 1999. *A Policy Framework for Consumer Protection in Electronic Commerce.* Canberra: Commonwealth of Australia.

Hockey, J. 2000. *Building Consumer Sovereignty in Electronic Commerce: A Best Practice Model for Business.* Canberra: Commonwealth of Australia.

Hogarth, J.M., and M.P. English. 2002. "Consumer Complaints and Redress: An Important Mechanism for Protecting and Empowering Consumers." *International Journal of Consumer Studies* 26, no. 3, pp. 217–226.

Internet Society. 2015. "Policy Brief: The Challenge of Spam." *Internet Society,* 30 October 2015. https://internetsociety.org/policybriefs/spam

Internet Society. 2017. *Cyber Security tops the list of concerns for Internet users in Asia-Pacific.* Singapore: Internet Society.

Interpol Global Complex for Innovation. 2020. *ASEAN Cyberthreat Assessment 2020: Key Insights from the ASEAN Cybercrime Operations Desk.* Singapore: Interpol Global Complex for Innovation.

Ismail, I. 2020. "Seven Cybercriminal Groups Targeting Southeast Asia Countries Identified." *New Straits Times*, 28 Feb 2020. https://nst.com.my/lifestyle/bots/2020/02/570070/tech-seven-cybercriminal-groups-targeting-southeast-asia-countries

Jackson, M. 2003. "Internet Privacy." *Telecommunications Journal of Australia* 53, no. 2, pp. 21–31.

Jawahitha, S. 2005. "Cyberjurisdiction and Consumer Protection in E-commerce." *Computer Law & Security Report* 21, no. 2, pp. 153–161.

Kehoe, C., J. Pitkow, K. Sutton, G. Aggarwal, and J.D. Rogers. 2006. "Results of GVU's Tenth World Wide Web User Survey 1999." http://gvu.gatech.edu/usersurveys/survey-1998-10/tenthreport.html.

Kierkegaard, M.S., and P. Kierkegaard. 2005. "What Women (Men) Want! E-consumer's Need and Right for Information." Paper read at The First International E-Business Conference, 23 - 25 June 2005, at Tunisia.

KPMG International Cooperative 2017. *The Truth About Online Consumers: 2017 Global Online Consumer Report.* KPMG International Cooperative.

Komiak, S.X., and I. Benbasat. 2004. "Understanding Customer Trust in Agent-Mediated Electronic Commerce, Web-Mediated Electronic Commerce, and Traditional Commerce." *Information Technology and Management* 5, no. 12, pp. 181–207.

Litman-Navarro, K. 2019. "We Read 150 Privacy Policies. They Were an Incomprehensible Disaster." *The New York Times*, June 12, 2019. https://nytimes.com/interactive/2019/06/12/opinion/facebook-google-privacy-policies.html

Liyanage, K.C. 2012. "The Regulation of Online Dispute Resolution: Effectiveness of Online Consumer Protection Guidelines." *Deakin Law Review* 172, pp. 251–282.

Lynch, E. 1997. "Protecting Consumers in the Cybermarket." *OECD Observer* 208, no. October/November 1997, pp. 11–15.

Mayer, R.N. 2002. "Shopping from a List: International Studies of Consumer Online Experiences." *Journal of Consumer Affairs* 36, no. 1, pp. 115–126.

Metz, C. 2005. "Identity Theft is Out of Control." *PC Magazine*, August 23, 2005, pp. 87–88.

Milloy, M., D. Fink, and R. Morris. 2002. "Modelling Online Security and Privacy to Increase Consumer Purchasing Intent." Paper read at Informing Science + IT Education Conference, 1921 June at Cork, Ireland.

Miyazaki, A.D., and A. Fernandez. 2001. "Consumer Perceptions of Privacy and Security Risks for Online Shopping." *Journal of Consumer Affairs* 35, no. 1, pp. 27–44.

Moghe, V. 2003. "Privacy Management - A New Era in the Australian Business Environment." *Information Management & Computer Security* 11, no. 2, pp. 60–66.

Molnar, A., and D. Harkin. 2019. *The Consumer Spyware Industry: An Australian-Based Analysis of the Threats of Consumer Spyware.* Deakin and Australian Communications Consumer Action Network (ACCAN).

Musuva, P.M.W., K.W Getao, and C.K. Chepken. 2019. "A New Approach to Modelling the Effects of Cognitive Processing and Threat Detection on Phishing Susceptibility." *Computers in Human Behavior* 94, pp. 154–175.

Norris, G., A. Brookes, and D. Dowell. 2019. "The Psychology of Internet Fraud Victimization: A Systematic Review." *Journal of Police and Criminal Psychology* 34, pp. 231–245.

Northern Territory Government of Australia. 2019. *Scams.* Northern Territory Government of Australia. https://nt.gov.au/law/crime/scams/ten-most-common-types-of-scams

NSW Office of Fair Trading. Undated. *International Consumer Rights: The World View on International Consumer Rights.* Parramatta: NSW Office of Fair Trading. https://fairtrading.nsw.gov.au/help-centre/youth-and-seniors/youth/international-consumer-rights

OECD. 2002a. "Civil Society and the OECD." *The Observer, OECD*, pp. 1–12.

OECD. 2002b. *Best Practice Examples under the OECD Guidelines on Consumer Protection in the Context of Electronic Commerce.* In *DSTI/CP2002)2/FINAL.* Paris: OECD.

OECD. 2002c. *Report on Consumer Protections for Payment Cardholders.* Paris: OECD.

OECD. 2006a. *Consumer Dispute Resolution and Redress in the Global Marketplace.* Paris: OECD.

OECD. 2006b. *Protecting Consumers from Cyberfraud.* Paris: OECD.

OECD. 2014. *Consumer Policy Guidance on Mobile and Online Payments.* OECD Digital Economy Papers, No. 236 (May 16, 2014). Paris: OECD Publishing. http://dx.doi.org/10.1787/5jz432cl1ns7-en

OECD. 2016. *Consumer Protection in E-commerce: OECD Recommendation.* Paris: OECD.

OECD. 2017. *OECD Digital Economy Outlook 2017.* Paris: OECD.

OECD. 2018. *Toolkit for Protecting Digital Consumers:* A Resource for G20 Policy Makers. Paris: OECD.

OECD. 2020. *OECD Policy Responses to Coronavirus (COVID-19): Protecting Online Consumers During the COVID-19 Crisis.* Paris: OECD. http://oecd.org/coronavirus/policy-responses/protecting-online-consumers-during-the-covid-19-crisis-2ce7353c/

Ong, C.E. 2005. "Jurisdiction in B2C E-Commerce redress in the European Community." *Journal of Electronic Commerce in Organizations* 3, no. 4, pp. 75–87.

Ong, C.E., and D. Teh. 2016. "Redress Procedures Expected by Consumers During a Business-To-Consumer E-Commerce Dispute." *Electronic Commerce Research and Applications* 17, no. May–June 2016, pp. 150–160.

Osterman, M. 2004. "Spim and Spam are Different Problems." *Network World*, May 4, 2004. https://networkworld.com/article/2332587/spim-and-spam-are-different-problems.html

Pace, E. 2020. "Consumer Privacy Takes Priority in 2020." *Forbes*, 18 February 2020. https://forbes.com/sites/forbestechcouncil/2020/02/18/consumer-privacy-takes-priority-in-2020/#28937b8e7abc

Perumal, V., and B. Shanmugam. 2004. "Internet Banking: Boon or Bane?" *Journal of Internet Banking and Commerce* 9, no. 3, pp. 1–6.

Pires, G.D., J. Stanton, and P. Rita. 2006. "The Internet, Consumer Empowerment and Marketing Strategies." *European Journal of Marketing* 40, no. 9/10, pp. 936–949.

Pratima, N., and G. Heggde. 2018. "A Critical Analysis of Consumer Protection in Social Media Selling with Reference to Information Disclosures." In *Social Media Marketing: Emerging Concepts and Applications*, eds. H. Githa, and G. Shainesh, 181193. Singapore: Spring Nature.

Purkait, S. 2012. "Phishing Counter Measures and their Effectiveness – Literature Review." *Information Management & Computer Security* 20, no. 5, pp. 382–420.

Scott, C. 2004. "Regulatory Innovation and the Online Consumer." *Law & Policy* 26, nos. 34, pp. 477–506.

Scottish Consumer Council. 2001. *E-Commerce and Consumer Protection: Consumers - Real Needs in a Virtual World*. Glasgow: Scottish Consumer Council.

Schlesinger, J., and A. Day. 2019. "Most People Just Click and Accept Privacy Policies Without Reading Them — You might be Surprised at What they Allow Companies to do." *CNBC*, February 9, 2019. https://cnbc.com/2019/02/07/privacy-policies-give-companies-lots-of-room-to-collect-share-data.html

Seçkin, G., D. Yeatts, S. Hughes, C. Hudson, and V. Bell. 2016. "Being an Informed Consumer of Health Information and Assessment of Electronic Health Literacy in a National Sample of Internet Users: Validity and Reliability of the e-HLS Instrument." *Journal of medical Internet research* 187, no. e161. https://doi.org/10.2196/jmir.5496

Stoney, M.A.S., and S. Stoney. 2003. "The Problems of Jurisdiction to E-commerce - Some Suggested Strategies." *Logistics Information Management* 16, no. 1, pp. 74–80.

Subirana, B., and M. Bain. 2005. *Consumer Protection. Legal Programming: Designing Legally Compliant RFID and Software Agent Architectures for Retail Processes and Beyond*. US: Springer.

Swinhoe, D. 2020. "Pharming Explained: How Attackers Use Fake Websites to Steal Data." CSO. April 23, 2020. https://csoonline.com/article/3537828/pharming-explained-how-attackers-use-fake-websites-to-steal-data.html

Tanodomdej, P. 2017. *E-Consumer Protection in ASEAN at the Crossroads: Challenges in the Harmonization of E-Commerce Law*. Bangkok: German-Southeast Asian Centre of Excellence for Public Policy and Good Governance (CPG).

The Age. 2007. "ID Theft Costs Australia $2b a Year." *The Age,* June 4, 2005. http://theage.com.au/news/Breaking/ID-theft-costs-Australia-2b-a-year/2005/06/03/11175683 609 68.html

UNCTAD. 2016. *Data Protection Regulations and International Data Flows: Implications for Trade and Development.* New York and Geneva: United Nations Conference on Trade and Development (UNCTAD).

UNCTAD. 2017. *Consumer Protection in Electronic Commerce.* New York, NY: United Nations Conference on Trade and Development (UNCTAD).

UNCTAD. 2018. *Dispute Resolution and Redress.* New York, NY: United Nations Conference on Trade and Development (UNCTAD).

Unisys. 2018. *2018 Unisys Security Index: Malaysia.* Unisys. https://www.unisys.com/ Style% 20Library/Unisys/usi2018/infographics/USI_Infographic_Malaysia.pdf

Unisys. 2019a. *2019 Unisys Security Index: Malaysia.* Unisys. https://unisys.com/ unisys-security-index-2019/malaysia

Unisys. 2019b. *2019 Unisys Security Index: Philippines.* Unisys. https://unisys. com/unisys-security-index-2019/philippines

Unisys 2020. *2020 Unisys Security Index: Consumers' Security Concerns Globally.* Unisys. https://assets.unisys.com/Documents/Microsites/USI2020/Unisys SecurityIndexReport2020.pdf?v=2

U.S. Consumer Product Safety Commission. 2019. *The Consumer Product Safety Improvement Act (CPSIA).* Bethesda, MD: Consumer Product Safety Commission.

U.S. Federal Trade Commission. 2019. *FTC Releases Results of 2017 Mass-Market Consumer Fraud Survey.* US Federal Trade Commission.

Ward, B.T., J. Sipior, and L. Volonino. 2016. "Internet Jurisdiction for E-commerce." *Journal of Internet Commerce* 15, no. 1, 117, doi: 10.1080/ 15332861. 2015.1109988

Weill, P., and M.R. Vitale. 2001. *Place to Space - Migrating to eBusiness Models.* Boston, Massachusetts: Harvard Business School Press.

Williams, B. 2019. "The dangers of password sharing at work." *TechRadar,* March 9, 2019. https://techradar.com/sg/news/the-dangers-of-password-sharing-at-work

World Economic Forum. 2019. The Global Governance of Online Consumer Protection and E-commerce Building Trust. Cologny/Geneva: World Economic Forum.

Yianakos, C. 2002. "Nameless in Cyberspace - Protecting Online Privacy." *B+FS,* December 2002, pp. 48–49.

Yuthayotin, S. 2014. *Access to Justice in Transnational B2C E-Commerce: A Multidimensional Analysis of Consumer Protection Mechanisms.* Springer International Publishing.

CHAPTER 3

The Current E-Consumer Protection Framework

Introduction

Currently, the issues associated with e-consumer protection have been addressed by a mixture of regulatory and nonregulatory measures at the national, regional, and international levels. Regulatory measures for e-consumer protection include "hard law," namely legislation/ acts and regulations; and "soft law," such as principles and guidelines that have been enacted by multilevel governments (World Economic Forum 2019). Such acts and regulations are mandatory and e-retailers must comply with them, and countries are encouraged to comply with international "soft law." Nonregulatory measures for e-consumer protection include codes of practice and guidelines from industry and consumer associations (civil society or the third sector) and internal policy and self-regulatory mechanisms by e-retailers (business or the second sector). Given the transient nature of the online market, e-consumer protection not only is a national issue, but has been transmuted to become one of the key supranational legal matters (Benöhr 2020; Howells, Ramsay and Wilhelmsson 2018). Thus, international and regional policy frameworks for e-consumer protection will also be briefly discussed in this chapter.

This chapter includes two main sections, excluding the conclusion. The first section discusses regulatory measures for e-consumer protection at the national, regional, and international levels. The next section explains how e-consumers are protected by nonregulatory measures by industry and/or trade associations, civil society organizations (CSOs, e.g., consumer associations), and e-retailers.

Regulatory Measures for E-Consumer Protection

Traditionally, regulation is defined as an attempt by an authority at the international, national, provincial, or local level to impose rules or directives that aim to control, influence, or change the behavior of individuals or groups in order to address the public interest (Baldwin and Cave 1999; Gow 1997). Such rules or directives are enforced by various mechanisms and supported by the use of rewards and punishment. Salazar (2007) defined regulation as

> An authoritative set of rules, accompanied by a mechanism— usually a public agency—for monitoring and promoting compliance with those rules. (p. 32)

Relevant authorities implement economic, social, and administrative regulation in order to achieve a set of socioeconomic, environmental, and political objectives (OECD 2000). Some regulations are used to encourage desirable behavior and activities of individuals, groups, or firms, whereas others discourage undesirable behavior and activities as well as prevent unwanted incidences (Baldwin and Cave 1999).

Regulation may be a single rule or a set of rules which are made by regulatory agencies and/or other authoritarian agencies (Baldwin and Cave 1999). There are two broad categories of regulation, namely (i) hard regulation, referring to legislation/acts, such as the TPA 1974 (Trade Practice Act 1974) of Australia or the *Consumer Protection (Fair Trading) Act (Cap. 52A)* of Singapore, and (ii) soft regulation, referring to international/ regional government guidelines, such as the *APEC Voluntary Online Consumer Protection Guidelines 2002*.[1] According to UNCTAD (undated), among 134 countries where data are available, 56 percent (110) of them have legislation related to e-consumer protection, 6 percent (8) are in the process of drafting relevant legislation, and 9 percent (12) have no

---

[1] Some authors use the term "soft regulation" to indicate "self-regulation" and preventive strategies, namely content regulation, certification and endorsement services, and information services (Sathye, Clark, and Dugdale, 2004).

legislation. Relevant data are not available in 57 countries (29 percent), and this suggests that e-consumer protection may not be addressed in these countries (UNCTAD undated).

The following section will discuss legislation/acts related to e-consumer protection at the national, regional, and international levels.

National Level

This section examines legislation enacted by ASEAN countries to protect e-consumers in the online market place. UNCTAD (undated) identified four categories of legislation that are related to e-consumer protection, namely electronic transactions, e-consumer protection, privacy and data protection, and cybercrime. From Table 3.1, we can see that all ASEAN countries have enacted electronic transactions legislation. Nine of them have legislation that can apply to e-consumer protection. Brunei has no such legislation. With regard to privacy and data protection, seven countries have relevant legislation, Myanmar has a draft one, and Brunei

Table 3.1 Legislation relevant to e-consumer protection in ASEAN countries (as of July 12, 2020)

Country	Electronic transactions	E-consumer protection	Privacy and data protection	Cybercrime
Brunei Darussalam	Y	N	N	Y
Cambodia	Y	Y	N	Draft
Indonesia	Y	Y	Y	Y
Laos People's Democratic Republic (Laos)	Y	Y	Y	Y
Malaysia	Y	Y	Y	Y
Myanmar	Y	Y	Draft	Draft
Philippines	Y	Y	Y	Y
Singapore	Y	Y	Y	Y
Thailand	Y	Y	Y	Y
Vietnam	Y	Y	Y	Y

Source: Adapted from UNCTAD (undated)

and Cambodia have no such legislation yet. Lastly, eight ASEAN countries have cybercrime-related acts, and two countries, Cambodia and Myanmar, are in the process of drafting such acts.

The electronic transaction-related acts cover issues related to the legal applications of and requirements for electronic data messages (ASEAN Secretariat 2018). As a result, e-transactions have the same status as other forms of traditional transactions, and thus an e-transaction must be treated in the same way as an offline transaction (Expert Group on Electronic Commerce (Australia) 2003). Such legislation mainly deals with "legal recognition of data messages" and e-contracts (Huffmann 2004, p. 11), not particularly dealing with consumer protection in e-retailing.

Nevertheless, most of the ASEAN member states have enacted consumer protection-related acts/legislation in recent years. Such legislation/acts are initially designed for consumers in the offline market, and e-consumers are covered in such legal documents as general "consumers." Many ASEAN countries acknowledge the importance of the protection of e-consumers in the online marketplace. Thus, they have revised the original consumer protection acts/legislation to include some provisions that apply specifically to e-consumer protection. The relevant legislation pertaining to e-consumer protection and the enforcement agencies of ASEAN countries are summarized in Table 3.2.

Table 3.2 Summary of e-consumer protection legislation and enforcement agencies of ASEAN countries

Country	E-consumer protection legislation	Enforcement agency
Brunei Darussalam	✓ *Consumer Protection (Fair Trading) Order 2011* (CPFTO) (passed in November 2011 and effective since January 1, 2012) ✓ *Electronic Transactions Act* (Chapter 196) 2000 (revised 2008) ✓ *Computer Misuse Order 2000* (Chapter 194) (amended in 2007)	✓ Competition and Consumer Affairs Department (CCAD), under the Department of Economic Planning and Development (JPKE), Prime Minister's Office ✓ Royal Brunei Police Force, Ministry of Communications ✓ Royal Brunei Police Force

Table 3.2 **(Continued)**

Cambodia	✓ *Consumer Protection Law* (passed and effective from November 2, 2019) ✓ *E-commerce Law* (effective from May 2020)	✓ National Committee for Consumer Protection (NCCP)
Indonesia	✓ *Law No. 8 of 1999 on Consumer Protection* (effective from April 20, 2000) ✓ *Information and Electronic Transaction Law No. 11/2008* ✓ *Government Regulation 80 of 2019 (GR 80, 2019)* ✓ *Consumer Protection Guidelines for ICT*	✓ Directorate of Consumer Empowerment, under the Directorate General of Consumer Protection and Trade Compliance, Ministry of Trade of Indonesia ✓ National Consumer Protection Agency (NCPA) ✓ Consumer Dispute Settlement Body (CDSB)
Laos People's Democratic Republic (Laos)	✓ *Consumer Protection Law No. 02/NA* (passed in June 2010, effective from September 2010) ✓ *Electronic Transactions Law, 2013* ✓ *Law on Prevention and Combating of Cybercrime 2015* ✓ *Electronic Data Protection Law 2017* (No. 25/NA, May 12, 2017)	✓ Ministry of Industry and Commerce (MOIC), Ministry of Health, Ministry of Agriculture and Forestry, and the Ministry of Science and Technology are in charge of enforcing consumer protection law ✓ Ministry of Science and Technology oversees e-commerce-related matters
Malaysia	✓ *Consumer Protection Act (CPA) 1999*, latest revision in April 2017 ✓ *Digital Signature Act 1997 (DSA 1997)* ✓ *Computer Crimes Act 1997* ✓ *Communications and Multimedia Act 1998* ✓ *Electronic Commerce Act 2006* ✓ *Consumer Protection (Electronic Trade Transactions) Regulations 2012* ✓ *Personal Data Protection Act 2010* (effective from January 1, 2013)	✓ Ministry of Domestic Trade, Co-operatives and Consumerism (MDTCC) ✓ The Malaysian Communications and Multimedia Commission administers the DSA 1997 ✓ Personal Data Protection Department
Myanmar	✓ *Electronic Transaction Law 2004* (amended in 2014) ✓ *Pyidaungsu Hluttaw Law No. 10/2014—Consumer Protection Law* (Burmese) (Enacted on March 14, 2014)	✓ Ministry of Communications and Information Technology (MCIT) ✓ Central Committee for Consumer Protection

Table 3.2 (Continued)

Philippines	✓ Consumer Act, 1992 (Republic Act No. 7394) (effective from July 15, 1992; RA 7394) ✓ E-Commerce Law of 2000 ✓ Joint DTI-DOH-DA Administrative Order No. 1 Series of 2008 ✓ Circulars No. 269 in 2000 and No. 542 in 2006 ✓ Data Privacy Act (2012) ✓ Cybercrime Prevention Act 2012 (or The Republic Act No. 10175)	✓ National Consumer Affairs Council (NCAC)
Singapore	✓ Consumer Protection (Fair Trading) Act 2003 (CPFTA) (the latest version in 2016) ✓ Lemon Law 2012 (part of the CPFTA) ✓ Electronic Transactions Act 2010 ✓ Electronic Transactions (Certification Authority) Regulations 2010 ✓ Personal Data Protection Act 2012 ✓ Computer Misuse Act 1993 (Chapter 50A) (revised in 2007)	✓ Competition and Consumer Commission of Singapore (CCCS) ✓ Infocomm Media Development Authority (IMDA) ✓ Personal Data Protection Commission
Thailand	✓ Consumer Protection Act 1979 (CPA) (goods) ✓ Consumer Protection Act of 1998 (services) ✓ Direct Sales and Direct Marketing Act 2002 (as amended in 2017) ✓ Product Liability Act 2008 ✓ Consumer Case Procedure Act 2008 ✓ Act on the Establishment of Consumer Organization Council Act 2019 ✓ Electronic Transaction Act BE.2544 2001 (effective from April 2019)	✓ Office of the Consumer Protection Board (OCPB) ✓ Electronic Transactions Development Agency (ETDA)

Table 3.2 (Continued)

Vietnam	✓ *Consumer Protection Law No. 59/2010/QH12* (2010) (enacted on November 15, effective from July 1, 2011) and Decree No. 99/2011/ ND-CP (on implementation of this law) ✓ *Electronic Communication Law No. 51/2005/QH11* (2005)	✓ Vietnam Competition and Consumer Authority (VCCA) ✓ Provincial Departments of Industry and Trade (DOITs) ✓ Ministry of Information and Communications (MIC)

Source: Compiled from ASEAN Secretariat (2018, 2020), APEC (2020, pp. 34–37), KPMG Cambodia Ltd. (2019), UNCTAD (2013), Department of Trade and Industry (undated), National Cyber Security Agency (2020), Johnson (2014), Malaysian Communications and Multimedia Commission (2020), UNCTAD (2018b), Consumers Association of Singapore (undated a), Chandran, R. (2004), *The Jakarta Post* (2019), and Le (2019).

Brunei Darussalam (Brunei)

The *Consumer Protection (Fair Trading) Order 2011 (CPFTO)* of Brunei Darussalam was enacted in November 2011 and effective from January 2012. Its scope covers both online and offline transactions, and it applies to all businesses or consumers residing in the country and online transactions (business-to-consumer, B2C) that originate in Brunei (Department of Economic Planning and Development (Brunei Darussalam) undated). The Competition and Consumer Affairs Department (CCAD), under the Department of Economic Planning and Development (JPKE) that is, in turn, under Prime Minister's Office, is in charge of consumer protection in Brunei (ASEAN Secretariat, 2018). Other relevant acts related to Internet services and e-commerce in Brunei are the *Sales of Good Act 1999*, the *Internet Code of Practice Notification 2001*, and the *AITI Order 2001* (to establish the Authority for Info-communications technology Industry [AITI]) (APEC 2020; ASEAN Secretariat 2018).

Brunei's *Electronic Transactions Act (Chapter 196)* was enacted in 2000 and revised in 2008. This act adopted several principles of the UNCITRAL Model Law on Electronic Commerce (1996) and includes provisions that aim to ensure the security of the cyberspace and promote the use of e-transactions, e-commerce, and e-communication (UNCTAD 2013). The Royal Brunei Police Force and the Ministry of Communications are the legal enforcers of this act (The Authority for Info-communications Technology Industry (Brunei) 2018).

The *Computer Misuse Order 2000 (Chapter 194)* (amended in 2007 and enforced by the Royal Brunei Police Force) of Brunei mirrors the 1993 *Electronic Transaction Act* of Singapore. This act aims to deter undesirable behaviors with regard to unauthorized access or modify information in a computer (The Authority for Info-communications Technology Industry (Brunei) 2018).

Cambodia

Cambodia passed two acts related to consumer protection on November 2, 2019, namely the *Consumer Protection Law* and the *E-commerce Law*, and they came into effect on November 2, 2019, and May 2, 2020, respectively (KPMG Cambodia Ltd. 2019). The *Consumer Protection Law* asserts the rights of consumers and regulates businesses' conduct with regard to fair trade practices. It applies to offline transactions within the country (Tilleke and Gibbins 2019). The National Committee for Consumer Protection (NCCP) is the enforcement authority overseeing consumer protection-related matters, including encouraging consumers to form consumer associations to protect their interests in various sectors/industries (KPMG Cambodia Ltd. 2019). The *E-commerce Law* aims to regulate domestic and cross-border online transactions in Cambodia and protect its e-consumers (Tilleke and Gibbins 2019).

Indonesia

Indonesia enacted the *Law No. 8 of 1999 on Consumer Protection* that came into effect on April 20, 2000 (UNCTAD 2019; ASEAN Secretariat 2018). This piece of legislation includes several provisions about the rights of consumers that are similar to those endorsed by the United Nations since 1985, for example, the right to security and safety in using and consuming products/services, the right to make choice, the right to receive information and to be heard, the right to redress, and the right to consumer education (Rohendi 2015). "The Directorate of Consumer

Empowerment, under the Directorate General of Consumer Protection and Trade Compliance, Ministry of Trade of Indonesia" is the enforcement authority of this act and is in charge of policy making, legal enforcement, and consumer education; it also handles consumer complaints (ASEAN Secretariat 2018, p. 29). The National Consumer Protection Agency (NCPA) and the Consumer Dispute Settlement Body (CDSB) are also responsible for promoting consumer protection in Indonesia (Consumers International 2011).

The *Information and Electronic Transaction Law No. 11/2008*, amended on October 27, 2016, recognizes the formation of an e-contract, recognizes e-signatures, and accepts e-evidence (Balfas 2009). This law includes article 26 that covers privacy issues, and articles 29 to 37 cover cybercrime-related provisions (UNCTAD 2013). However, *Regulation Number 82 of 2012 Concerning Electronic System and Transaction Operation* does contain more privacy requirements in order to protect personal data of users (UNCTAD 2013). Another document, Indonesia's *Consumer Protection Guidelines for ICT*, states that consumers should have the rights to choose products, providers, and services; and their privacy information must be respected and protected (ASEAN Secretariat 2018).

The latest legislation passed by Indonesia is the *Government Regulation 80 of 2019 (GR 80, 2019)*, effective from November 2021, that aims to enhance the governance of e-transactions, and businesses are required to adhere to the requirements with regard to business address, e-contracts, e-transactions, and the provisions for consumer right protection (Medina 2020; *The Jakarta Post* 2019).

Laos People's Democratic Republic (Laos)

Laos passed the *Consumer Protection Law No. 02/NA* in June 2010, and it came to effect in September 2010. This law includes 9 parts and 74 articles, "the first of its kind in this area" (ASEAN Secretariat 2018, p. 30). However, it also applies to offline transactions (UNCTAD 2018b). According to this act, four ministries, namely Ministry of Industry and Commerce (MOIC), Ministry of Health, Ministry of Agriculture and Forestry, and Ministry of Science and Technology, are in charge of enforcing consumer protection law (ASEAN Secretariat 2018).

The *Electronic Transactions Law 2013* aims to recognize the legality of e-signatures, e-contracts, and e-transactions in order to develop the full potential of e-commerce and promote a safe cyber environment for all users. It aims to "protect the rights and interests of both cyber-service and electronic information service providers and users" (Sengpunya 2019, p. 382), but does not supersede the *Consumer Protection Law*. The Ministry of Science and Technology oversees e-commerce-related matters (ASEAN Secretariat 2018). The *Law on Prevention and Combating of Cybercrime 2015* was passed on July 15, 2015. It aims to prevent and combat cyber-crimes and protect cyber users (Sengpunya 2019). Laos also passed the *Electronic Data Protection Law 2017* (No. 25/NA, May 12, 2017) in 2017, and it took effect in October 2017. It includes some provision aiming to protect personal data of individuals and groups (Cruz 2018).

Malaysia

Malaysia's *Digital Signature Act 1997* (DSA 1997) was passed earlier than the *Consumer Protection Act 1999* and came into effect on October 1, 1998. It aims to provide an avenue for secure e-transactions via the acceptance of digital signatures and is administered by the Malaysian Communications and Multimedia Commission (MCMC) (2020). In the same year, Malaysia also introduced the *Computer Crimes Act 1997*, but effective only from June 1, 2000. It aims to deter the misuse of computers, including unauthorized access to or modify computer data/contents and intention to commit other offences (National Cyber Security Agency 2020).

Malaysia enacted the *Consumer Protection Act (CPA) 1999* several years ago, applied to traditional commerce. It aims to complement other major legislations in terms of consumer protection. The CPA has been amended many times, and the latest revision was on April 26, 2017, covering several emerging issues related to e-consumer protection and unfair contract terms and conditions (ASEAN Secretariat 2018). The Ministry of Domestic Trade and Consumer Affairs (MDTCA) of Malaysia is responsible for legal enforcement of consumer protection, and handles consumers' complaints. It also supports the National Consumer Advisory Council (NCAC) (under the MDTCA) which advises the Minister of MDTCA on consumer-related issues and the implementation of the CPA (Malaysia Ministry of Domestic Trade and Consumer Affairs 2020).

The *Electronic Commerce Act 2006* (ECA 2006) was introduced by Malaysia to provide legal recognition of e-messages and put in place legal requirements that mandate a provider to provide all necessary information so that consumers can make informed decisions before committing to an e-contract (Ayub, Yusoff and Sharif 2007). The ECA 2006 has mirrored some key principles of the United Nations Electronic Communications Convention (ecInsider 2014). This act has been complemented by the enactment of the *Personal Data Protection Act (PDPA) 2010* by Malaysia that was effective from January 1, 2013. The PDPA 2010 has adapted some principles in the European Union directive on personal data protection and some guidelines of the APEC Privacy Framework (ecInsider 2014).

Compared to other countries, Malaysia has introduced more regulations/acts to protect e-consumers. One of the key legislations is the *Consumer Protection (Electronic Trade Transactions) Regulations 2012* that was enforced in 2013 (UNCTAD 2013). These regulations require e-retailers and other online operators to comply with the government regulations that can enhance e-consumers' trust and confidence in e-retailing. The *Communications and Multimedia Act 1998* also includes some consumer protection provisions (Part 8) applied to both offline and online transactions. Service providers are obliged to provide redress mechanisms to consumers as well as to address consumers' complaints (UNCTAD 2013).

Myanmar

Myanmar's *Electronic Transaction Law 2004* was enacted in 2004 and revised in 2014. It is administered and enforced by the Ministry of Communications and Information Technology (MCIT) (ASEAN Secretariat 2018). This act regulates e-contracts and stipulates some cyber offences that aim to deter cybercrimes. It also aims to establish a number of regulatory authorities, including (i) the Central Body of Electronic Transactions that is responsible for legal enforcement of this act and (ii) the Electronic Transactions Control Board that is in charge of the governance of e-signatures (UNCTAD 2013).

Enacted on March 14, 2014, the *Pyidaungsu Hluttaw Law No. 10/2014—Consumer Protection Law* of Myanmar aims to address consumer-related issues, in general, not specific to e-consumer protection

(Johnson 2014). It includes provisions on dispute resolution and penalty for noncompliance. Similar to the consumer protection law of Indonesia, this act stipulates the rights of consumers to safety and seeking redress if they have valid evidence (Kyaw 2014). The Central Committee for Consumer Protection was also established by this act, comprising the Minister of Commerce, representatives of other ministries, and CSOs (e.g., consumer groups) (Johnson 2014).

Philippines

The *Consumer Act, 1992 (Republic Act No. 7394 or RA 7394)* of the Philippines was adopted on July 15, 1992. The RA 7394 aims to protect consumers' interests and enhance consumer protection, in general, by establishing standards of conduct for business and industry to comply with (ASEAN Secretariat 2018). This act also includes the establishment of the National Consumer Affairs Council (NCAC). The NCAC, consisting of representatives from government and nongovernment organizations (e.g., Department of Education, Department of Trade and Industry, Department of Health, Department of Agriculture, consumer organizations, and the private sector), oversee and coordinate consumer-related matters (ASEAN Secretariat 2018).

The Philippines also passed the *Electronic Commerce Act 2000* (ECA 2000) of which many provisions are adopted from the UNCITRAL Model Law on Electronic Commerce (1996) (UNCTAD 2013). It legally recognized e-documents and e-messages created for both commercial and noncommercial transactions and stipulates penalties for noncompliance (UNCTAD 2013). E-consumers are protected by an order related to the ECA 2000, that is, the *JOINT DTI-DOH-DA Administrative Order No. 1 Series of 2008.* This order applies to both local and international e-retailers (Department of Trade and Industry, undated). Other orders, *Circulars No. 269 in 2000* and *No. 542 in 2006*, were introduced by the Central Bank of the Philippines (BSP) to cover online banking transactions, protect customers' personal information, and prevent money laundering (Bangko Sentral ng Pilipinas undated).

Additionally, the Philippines enacted the *Data Privacy Act 2012 (DPA 2012)* that is considered as "one of the most modern privacy laws in the region, incorporating a mix of guidance from the European Union, APEC and OECD" (UNCTAD 2013, p. 35). This act aims to protect personal information of individuals and applies to the public and private sectors. This act also stipulates that individuals have the right of privacy and of communication (National Privacy Commission (Philippines) undated).

The *Cybercrime Prevention Act 2012* (or The *Republic Act No. 10175*) stipulates the establishment of the Cybercrime Investigation and Coordinating Centre, under the Department of Information and Communications Technology, that is responsible for cybersecurity-related matters (Department of Information and Communications Technology (Philippines), undated). Together with this act, some provisions of the Philippines *Electronic Commerce Act 2000* also deal with cyber offences, namely "hacking, cracking, or unauthorized access using a computer in order to corrupt, alter, steal or destroy electronic data are all offences" (UNCTAD 2013, p. 36).

Singapore

Singapore enacted the *Consumer Protection (Fair Trading) Act* (CPFTA) in November 2003, including many provisions adopted from consumer protection laws in many Commonwealth jurisdictions (ASEAN Secretariat 2018). This act came into effect in March 2004 and was revised many times. The latest revision of the act was in 2016. This act was originally adopted to protect consumers against unfair trade practices in traditional commerce, not specifically for e-consumers. Nevertheless, some provisions of this act are relevant to e-transactions (Chandran 2004). From April 1, 2018, the Competition and Consumer Commission of Singapore (CCCS) has been responsible for administering the CPFTA, whereas CASE (Consumers Association of Singapore) and the Singapore Tourism Board are appointed to handle complaints by local consumers and tourists, respectively (Consumers Association of Singapore undated a). In addition, Singapore also introduced the *Lemon Law* (sections 12A to 12F of the CPFTA), effective from September 1, 2012, that "protects consumers against goods that do not conform to contract or are not of satisfactory quality or performance standards at the time of delivery" (Consumers Association of Singapore undated a, para. 14). Under this law, businesses are responsible to take corrective action, such as repairing, replacing, giving discount, providing a refund or an exchange, for a defective good (Lau 2017).

Singapore's *Electronic Transactions Act (CAP 88)* and the *Electronic Transactions (Certification Authority) Regulations 2010* were enacted in 1998 (and re-enacted in 2010) and 2010, respectively. These acts aim to protect consumers in terms of providing assurance of security and certainty for the adoption of e-transactions. The Infocomm Media Development Authority (IMDA) is the enforcement agency of these acts (ASEAN Secretariat 2018).

The *Personal Data Protection Act 2012 (PDPA)* was passed by the government of Singapore in 2012. The Personal Data Protection Commission is responsible for the administration and implementation of this act. This piece of legislation aims to provide protection for personal data across sectors in the economy and is complementing "sector-specific legislative and regulatory frameworks," that is, organizations must comply with the PDPA as well as other relevant laws with regard to collecting, using, storing, and retrieving personal information (Personal Data Protection Commission undated).

The *Computer Misuse Act 1993* (Chapter 50A) of Singapore, revised in 2007, contains offence provisions that apply to unauthorized access and use of computers and computer-related technology (Urbas 2008). It aims to deter (i) unauthorized access, use, and/or modification of computers, programs, and data stored in such computers and (ii) authorized or unauthorized access, modification, and use of computers and their content for an intention to commit crimes (Urbas 2008; UNCTAD 2013).

Thailand

The *Consumer Protection Act 1979* (CPA) (goods) and the *Consumer Protection Act of 1998* (services) of Thailand aim to protect consumers in traditional commerce. They were revised many times to incorporate more protection for consumers, and the latest revision was in 2019 (ASEAN Secretariat 2020a; Nethin 2010). Thailand takes consumer issues seriously. Thus, Thailand instituted the Office of the Consumer Protection Board (OCPB), chaired by the prime minister and supervised by the Office of the Prime Minister, in July 1979. The OCPB is responsible for handling consumer complaints and provides various redress mechanisms (Thailand Law Forum 2009). It also handles mediation and acts on behalf of consumers by bringing offending cases to court (ASEAN Secretariat 2018).

Other consumer protection-related legislations include the *Direct Sales and Direct Marketing Act 2002* (revised in 2017), the *Product Liability Act 2008*, the *Consumer Case Procedure Act 2008*, and the *Act on the Establishment of Consumer Organization Council Act 2019* (ASEAN Secretariat 2018). Yet, all of these acts do not specifically protect e-consumers.

Thailand's *Electronic Transaction Act BE. 2544 (2001),* effective from April 2019, aims to improve consumer confidence in e-commerce by legally recognizing e-information and e-transactions (Nethin 2010). This act requires businesses that want to offer services related to e-transactions to have a physical presence (branch or representative office) in Thailand in normal conditions (Mendiola 2019). The Electronic Transactions Development Agency (ETDA) formulates policies and regulations to promote e-transactions as well as monitors business operations of e-transactions (Chanpanich and Mahakunkitchareon 2019).

Thailand also enacted the *Computer Crime Act, B.E. 2550* (2007) and the *Amendment B.E. 2560* (2016) that adopts the main principles of the Budapest Convention on Cybercrime (UNCTAD 2013). Similar to cybercrime-related acts of other ASEAN countries, these laws aim to deter the use of computers for committing crimes by stipulating offences committed against a computer or its content (UNCTAD 2013).

The recent *Personal Data Protection Act B.E. 2562 (2019)* (PDPA) was enacted by the Thai Government on May 27, 2019; yet, it only took effect partially on the next day. It means that many provisions relating to the operations and "the rights of a data subject, the obligations of a data controller and the penalties for non-compliance" only came into effect one year later, that is, on May 27, 2020 (Kiratisountorn et al. 2020, para.1). Thailand's PDPA provides for three types of potential liability, namely civil, criminal, and administrative liability, for violation of its provisions (*Bangkok Post* 2019). In Thailand, the Office of Data Protection Committee, under the Ministry of Digital Economy and Society, administers the PDPA and is responsible for privacy-related matters, such as collection, storage, usage, and disclosure of personal information within and outside the country (Kiratisountorn et al. 2020).

Vietnam

The *Consumer Protection Law* No. 59/2010/QH12 *(2010) (CPL)* was enacted by Vietnam's National Assembly in November 2010 and took effect from July 2011. This law replaced the *1999 Ordinance on Protection of Consumers' Rights. Decree No. 99/2011/ND-CP* issued by the Government of Vietnam aims to provide guidance to stakeholders on the implementation of the CPL (ASEAN Secretariat 2018). At the national level, the Vietnam Competition and Consumer Authority (VCCA) is the enforcement agency of the CPL 2010. At the provincial level, the respective Departments of Industry and Trade (DOITs) are in charge of consumer protection-related matters and work with businesses to resolve consumer complaints, including e-consumers' complaints (Ministry of Industry and Trade, Vietnam Competition and Consumer Authority 2019).

The *Electronic Communication Law* No. 51/2005/QH11 *(2005)* of Vietnam was passed in 2005 and was administered by the Ministry of Information and Communications (MIC). This law aims to regulate e-transactions by the public and private sectors, business, and CSO (ASEAN Secretariat 2018, Le 2019).

The *Law on Cybersecurity No. 24/2018/QH14* was enacted on June 12, 2018, by Vietnam's National Assembly. This law aims to regulate activities in the cyberspace in order to protect the legal rights and interests of individuals, organizations, national security, and public order in the online platforms. It stipulates various measures to protect cybersecurity, for example, "cybersecurity appraisal; cybersecurity assessment; cybersecurity inspection; cybersecurity monitoring; cybersecurity incident response and remediation; cybersecurity protection activities; use of cryptography for cybersecurity protection" and others (Ministry of Justice (Vietnam) 2018, para. 3).

Vietnam, given the increasing number of personal data thefts, is also in the process of passing a governmental decree pertaining to personal data protection that aims to safeguard individuals' and organizations' information (*The Star Online* 2020).

Overall, most of the ASEAN countries have enacted consumer protection-related laws, but not specifically for e-consumer protection. Consumer protection regulations also differ significantly among ASEAN member states due to different legislative environment and development. For instance, "Brunei Darussalam, Indonesia, Malaysia, Singapore, Thailand and Viet Nam have adopted their consumer protection laws to include special provisions to deal with e-commerce," whereas consumer protection laws of other countries apply to general consumers (APEC 2020, p. 37).

Regional Level

Regional principles, guidelines, and legislation on e-consumer protection are examined in this section.

ASEAN

In 2000, ASEAN member states discussed and concluded an *e-ASEAN Framework Agreement* (15 articles), including the conceptualization of e-consumer protection. The main objective of this agreement is to promote cooperation among ASEAN state members, and between the public and private sectors, to develop a competitive ICT sector in ASEAN and to materialize e-ASEAN (ASEAN Secretariat 2012). Member states have agreed to enact e-commerce regulatory and legislative frameworks that can enhance e-consumer protection (*Tanodomdej 2017*).

Apart from the *e-ASEAN Framework Agreement*, the ASEAN ICT Masterplans 2015 (2011 to 2015) and 2020 (2016 to 2020) and the introduction of the *Master Plan on ASEAN Connectivity 2025* offer opportunities for strengthening e-consumer protection in ASEAN (ASEAN Secretariat 2017; *Tanodomdej 2017*).

In 2018, ASEAN Secretariat (2018) introduced the *Handbook on ASEAN Consumer Protection Laws and Regulation*, including the regional framework for protection of consumers. This framework applies to consumers in all forms of commerce, not specifically to e-consumers. However, this handbook does include ASEAN High-Level (AHL) principles of consumer protection. AHL Principle 8 clearly states that consumers in e-commerce should be protected. The ASEAN regional framework for consumer protection includes three main components:

(a) *The ASEAN Committee on Consumer Protection (ACCP)*: This committee was formed in 2007 by the ASEAN Economic Ministers (AEM). The committee consists of delegates from various agencies in charge of consumer protection in ten ASEAN countries. Its function is to coordinate and oversee the implementation and monitor "regional arrangements and mechanisms to foster consumer protection in the ASEAN Economic Community (AEC)" (*ASEAN* Secretariat 2018, p. 13).

(b) *The ASEAN Strategic Action Plan on Consumer Protection (ASAPCP)* from 2016 to 2025: This plan aims to develop a common framework for consumer protection in ASEAN member states by enacting legislation, improving legal enforcement, and making available redress mechanisms. It also promotes measures to protect consumers in various sectors, including e-retailing (*ASEAN* Secretariat 2018, p. 13).

(c) *ASEAN High-Level Principles on Consumer Protection*: There are eight AHL principles that aim to provide ASEAN member states with a clear direction to establish a macro framework on consumer protection for member countries (*ASEAN* Secretariat 2018, p. 14).

Among these principles, Principle 8 focuses on e-consumer protection. Principle 8 requests ASEAN member states to enact new legislation, if necessary, and review and amend current legislation to protect e-consumers. These countries should also oversee the implementation of such legislations to ensure effective e-consumer protection. E-consumers should be informed and educated about security and privacy risk, and measures to mitigate such risk when they transact online. This principle also calls for ASEAN countries to establish dispute resolution mechanisms, including online mechanisms, to "handle cross-border transactions and provide the consumers with fair outcomes" (*ASEAN* Secretariat 2018, p. 15).

Asia Pacific Economic Cooperation (APEC)

At the regional level, apart from the principles and guidelines issued by ASEAN, the APEC Electronic Commerce Steering Group (ECSG) introduced the *APEC Guidelines for Consumer Protection* in e-retailing (APEC

Electronic Commerce Steering Group 2007). The guidelines cover a wide range of areas related to e-consumer protection, such as international and regional cooperation, education, awareness enhancement, advertisement and marketing, and dispute resolutions (Heseltine 2007). Security and privacy are considered the key challenges in e-retailing and should receive more attention (Heseltine 2007). These guidelines cover areas that are similar to those issued by the UN and the OECD and are in line with the eight basic consumer rights.

APEC also published a number of documents that promote consumer protection in the online marketplace. For example, the APEC *Cross-Border E-Commerce Facilitation Framework* acknowledges that e-consumer protection is particularly important for businesses engaging in cross-border e-commerce and encourages member countries to strengthen cooperation between the public and private sectors to promote e-consumer protection (APEC undated). The *APEC Blueprint for Action on Electronic Commerce* also advises the public and private sectors to work closely with each other to develop policies and adopt technologies that can enhance trust and confidence in the online marketplace in order to address issues associated with privacy, authentication, and e-consumer protection (APEC 1998). The establishment of the Digital Economy Steering Group (DESG) in 2018 demonstrates APEC leaders' commitment to work with one another to materialize the full potential of a digital economy. The proposed *APEC Internet and Digital Economy Roadmap* also highlights the need for collaboration among member countries to "promote a regulatory approach that provides appropriate legitimate consumer protection to enable the flow of information and data" (APEC 2017, p. 5).

International Level

International principles, guidelines, and legislation on e-consumer protection are summarized in Table 3.3.

United Nations (UN)

The *United Nations Guidelines for Consumer Protection* (1985) was initially introduced for consumers in traditional commerce. This set of guidelines was implemented in 1985 (Harland 1987), strengthening the UN basic consumer rights. These guidelines provide member countries with clear direction pertaining to developing and revising (if necessary) national regulatory frameworks and policies to enhance consumer protection (Ha 2011, 2012, 2017). The UN guidelines emphasize two key concerns, namely (i) "the imbalance that consumers face in economic terms, educational levels and bargaining power"; and (ii) "the importance of promoting just, equitable and sustainable economic and social development" that should be tackled at both the international and national levels (Qaqaya 2012, p. 3).

These guidelines were revised twice: 1999 and 2015. The latest *United Nations Guidelines for Consumer Protection ("UN Guidelines")*, effective from 2015, aim to enhance the awareness of the public sector, the private sector (businesses), and the third sector (civil society) that can, in turn, improve consumer protection (United Nations 2016). This document specifically asserted that the level of protection for e-consumers should not be less than the one for consumers in other forms of commerce, as follows:

> A level of protection for consumers using electronic commerce that is not less than that afforded in other forms of commerce. (United Nations 2016, p. 8)

This document of the UN advises countries to develop effective consumer protection policies if there are no such policies, or revise the existing consumer protection policies that are relevant to consumers in e-retailing. In this case, the UN guidelines have been revised to cover the protection for consumers in both traditional commerce and e-retailing. Section XII in the *Manual on Consumer Protection* by the UNCTAD (2018a) affirmed the legitimate need of e-consumers stated in the *UN Guidelines*, that is, to ensure e-consumers receive the same level of protection when they are online. The scope of the protection has also been extended from B2C (business-co-consumer) to C2C (consumer-to-consumer).

The UN has also introduced a number of resolutions to fight against the misuse of information technologies for unlawful activities (e.g., *Resolution 55/63* and *Resolution 56/121*). The UN also calls for member

countries to create a culture of cybersecurity and emphasizes the importance of the protection of critical information infrastructures (Resolutions 57/239 and 58/199) (Cornelius 2006). These resolutions are further
extended by the *Resolution 64/211 (2010)*, asserting that member countries must work with stakeholders to protect critical information infrastructures, and calling for international collaboration to support national
effort (United Nations 2010). The UN's *Resolution 57/239* (2003) affirms
that cybersecurity is one of "the main pillars of the information society"
(Dunn 2005, p. 1). Finally, the UN (2014) reaffirms the human right
to privacy by adopting *Resolution 68/167 (2013)*. Accordingly, nobody
should interfere in others' privacy, and everyone is rightly protected
against such privacy interference.

Overall, for the purpose of this volume, only some key resolutions and
documents relevant to e-consumer protection are discussed and included
in Table 3.3. These documents published by the UN, the OECD, and the
EU provide directions and suggestions to member countries in order to
address the protection of consumers in both the offline and online markets. Also, it should be noted that these principles of and guidelines for
e-consumer protection are suggested, not mandatory.

The Organization for Economic Co-operation and Development (OECD)

The OECD *Guidelines for Consumer Protection in the Context of Electronic
Commerce* (1999) *("OECD Guidelines")*, adopted by the OECD Council
in 1999, includes eight principles as shown in Table 3.4 (Ha 2011, 2012,
2107; OECD 2000; Smith 2004). It also covers the scope (B2C, not B2B),
the implementation of these guidelines, and global cooperation to protect
e-consumers. These *guidelines* aim to safeguard e-consumers' interest in
the online market and to facilitate e-retailing by promoting fair business
practices, good advertising and marketing practices, transparent information disclosure and process, and encouraging private sector initiatives. It
also calls for cooperation among all groups of stakeholders, namely the
public sector, businesses, and civil societies (OECD 2000). Similar to the
UN, the OECD adopts these guidelines to establish a foundation for its
member countries to review and revise the existing national e-consumer

Table 3.3 International principles and guidelines for e-consumer protection

UN (United Nations)	OECD (Organization for Economic Co-operation and Development)
• United Nations Guidelines for Consumer Protection 1985 (expanded in 1999) • United Nations Guidelines for Consumer Protection 2015 • UNCTAD Manual on consumer protection (2018a) • Resolution 55/63, January 2001: Combating the criminal misuse of information technologies • Resolution 56/121, January 2002: Combating the criminal misuse of information technologies • Resolution 57/239, January 2003: Creation of a global culture of cybersecurity • Resolution 58/199, January 2004: Creation of a global culture of cybersecurity and the protection of critical information infrastructures • Resolution 64/211, March 2010: Creation of a global culture of cybersecurity and taking stock of national efforts to protect critical information infrastructures • Resolution 68/167 (2013), The right to privacy in the digital age	• Guidelines for Consumer Protection in the Context of Electronic Commerce 1999, revised in 2016 and replaced by Consumer Protection in E-commerce: OECD Recommendation (2016) • OECD Guidelines on the Protection of Privacy and Transborder Flows of Personal Data 1980, revised in 2013 • OECD Policy Guidance on Online Identity Theft (2008) • Guidelines for the Security of Information Systems and Networks: Towards a Culture of Security (2002) replaced by Recommendation of the Council on Digital Security Risk Management for Economic and Social Prosperity (2015) • OECD Recommendation on Consumer Dispute Resolution and Redress (2007) • Report on Consumer Dispute Resolution and Redress in the Global Marketplace (2006) • Resolving E-retailing Disputes Online: Asking the Right Questions about ADR (2002) • OECD Guidelines for Protecting Consumers from Fraudulent and Deceptive Commercial Practices Across Borders (2003) • Consumer Protection Enforcement in a Global Digital Marketplace (2018)

Sources: Compiled from Cauffman (2019), Dunn (2005), Ha (2012, 2017), Ha and Coghill (2008), Ha, Coghill and Maharaj (2009), Harland (1987), ITU (2020), OECD (2002b), OECD (2003b), World Economic Forum (2019)

protection legislation and practices in order to harmonize the level of protection of consumers in the online and offline markets (OECD, 2000, 2019; Smith, 2004). This, in turn, would improve e-consumers' trust in e-retailing (UNCTAD 2017).

Table 3.4 shows that the OECD guidelines consist of eight principles which reflect the five basic consumer rights. The third and fourth OECD

Table 3.4 The OECD guidelines for e-consumer protection (1999)

Guideline	OECD guidelines
1	Transparent and effective protection
2	Fair business, advertising, and marketing practices
3	Online disclosures information about the business, the goods or services, the transaction
4	Confirmation process
5	Payment
6	Dispute resolution and redress
7	Privacy
8	Education and awareness

Source: Summarized from OECD (2000b)

guidelines refer to the second and third basic consumer rights, that is, the right "to choose" and to obtain information about the business, goods and services, and the transaction. The OECD guidelines relating to payment and privacy reflect the first basic consumer right "to safety" in terms of online security and privacy. The sixth and eighth OECD principles affirm the rights of consumers to seek redress and to receive education, respectively.

The *OECD Guidelines* were revised in 2016 and replaced by the *Consumer Protection in E-commerce: OECD Recommendation 2016.* The OECD's revised recommendations aim to deal with new challenges pertaining to e-consumer protection. Given new developments in e-retailing, the following new recommendations are included in the revised version, namely nonmonetary transactions, digital content products, active consumers, mobile devices, privacy and security risk, payment protection, and product safety (OECD 2016). For example, with regard to nonmonetary transactions, redress mechanisms should be provided to consumers who experience problems with nonmonetary transactions when obtaining complementary "goods and services in exchange for their personal data" (OECD 2016, p. 4). These areas have been identified as the main issues associated with e-consumer protection in the previous chapter.

Regarding privacy, the *OECD Guidelines on the Protection of Privacy and Transborder Flows of Personal Data*, introduced in 1980 and revised in 2013, advise OECD member countries to adopt a wide range of measures to deal with privacy incidents, such as using (i) market-based incentives and punishment (e.g., trust-marks and seals) to encourage compliance with standards, (ii) technical measures (e.g., to P3P), (iii) a self-regulatory approach (e.g., online privacy policies), and (iv) online privacy-related dispute resolution (Ha 2012; Ha, et al. 2009; OECD 2003c). The revised guidelines focus on the practical application of privacy protection laws and regulations, incorporating risk management, and call for more concerted efforts to tackle the global nature of privacy (OECD 2013). Given the rapid development of privacy issues, this revised set of guidelines introduced the following three new concepts:

1. National privacy strategies: A multidimensional national strategy and high-level coordination among various levels of government are required to address privacy issues;
2. Privacy management programs: Countries should have clear programs, including operational mechanisms that can help organizations implement privacy protection; and
3. Data security breach notification: The relevant authority and individuals who are affected by a security breach of privacy should be notified timely (OECD 2013).

Concerning security, the *OECD Guidelines for the Security of Information Systems and Networks: towards a Culture of Security* adopted in 2002 encourage member countries to introduce and implement self-regulatory measures to ensure online security for all e-users. In 2003, the implementation of these OECD guidelines was reported in a document entitled *The Implementation Plan for the OECD Guidelines for the Security of Information Systems and Networks: Towards a Culture of Security*. This document highlights the roles of different groups of stakeholders (e.g., government, e-retailers, and CSOs) to take collective responsibility to solve global security issues because they are the owners, users, and operators of the global information systems and networks (OECD 2003b). These OECD guidelines were revised and replaced by another document, that is, *Recommendation of the Council on Digital Security Risk Management for Economic and Social Prosperity* (2015). This document covers two key notes: (i) member countries should treat digital risk as socioeconomic risk and as an essential element of the overall risk management framework and decision-making processes of organizations and (ii) the design of online security measures should take into consideration the interests of stakeholders and does not undermine relevant socioeconomic activities that it aims to protect (OECD 2015).

The report on *Resolving E-retailing Disputes Online: Asking the Right Questions about ADR* (2002), and the *OECD Guidelines for Protecting Consumers from Fraudulent and Deceptive Commercial Practices Across Borders* (2003) outline the work of the OECD's Committee on Consumer Policy regarding cross-border redress (OECD 2006a). The *OECD Recommendation on Consumer Dispute Resolution and Redress* (2007) was designed and adopted for domestic and cross-border transactions (i.e., offline and online transactions), and it is specifically useful to countries given the rapid development of e-retailing (OECD 2007). This document includes seven parts, and part III specifies cross-border consumer disputes. It calls for member countries to have redress mechanisms in place, and enhance consumers' awareness of and access to various dispute resolution mechanisms in order to improve "the effectiveness of consumer remedies in cross-border disputes" (OECD 2007, p. 11).

Another document, the OECD report on *Consumer Dispute Resolution and Redress in the Global Marketplace* (2006), discusses the seven main mechanisms available to consumers for seeking redress, namely (i) internal complaints handling processes, (ii) payment cardholder protections, (iii) alternative dispute resolution, (iv) small claims courts, (v) private collective action lawsuits, (vi) legal actions by consumer associations, and (vii) government-obtained redress (OECD 2006a). It also analyzes obstacles faced by consumers when they want to obtain monetary compensation from overseas e-retailers, and encourages collective efforts of intergovernmental organizations to develop mechanisms to address cross-jurisdiction disputes and redress.

A recent document published by the OECD is *Consumer Protection Enforcement in a Global Digital Marketplace 2018*. This document reviews activities of consumer protection enforcement authorities of both member and nonmember countries (OECD, 2018). The findings propose that there have been some forms of cross-country cooperation, but such cooperation is still limited and applies among few countries. Many factors affect the implementation and effectiveness of international collaboration, for example, lack of resources, lack of legal authority, lack of legal enforcement and inconsistent legal frameworks, confidentiality rules and restriction of privacy and data protection (OECD 2018).

Nonregulatory Measures for E-Consumer Protection

Nonregulatory measures include (i) codes of practice and/or guidelines by industry associations and consumer associations and (ii) internal policy and self-regulatory mechanisms by e-retailers.

Industry Associations

Codes of conduct are practical starting points for the standards of corporate behavior because they can minimize unethical and unfair trading practice and can enhance e-consumers' trust in e-retailing (ASEAN Secretariat 2018). Any breach of these codes will affect the reputation and performance of individual corporations and the entire industry in which the corporations operate. The establishment and compliance with benchmarks can also help organizations to fulfill their legal, economic, and social responsibilities, and industry associations/organizations can affect their members with regard to compliance with government regulation (Mendoza, Dekker and Wielhouwer 2020; Lahey 2005). In e-retailing, codes of conduct sets norms for consumer protection in areas where "the special characteristics" of e-retailing create challenges "not usually encountered in the traditional retail environment" (Expert Group on Electronic Commerce (Australian Government) 2003, p. 5). These benchmarks are aimed to establish consumer sovereignty in e-retailing, including the ability of e-consumers to make independent and well-informed decisions through understanding of their consumer rights when transacting online, and accessibility to effectual redress mechanisms which are supported by a robust regulatory framework for e-consumer protection (Expert Group on Electronic Commerce (Australian Government) 2003). Adoption of a code of conduct also demonstrates e-retailers' responsible business conduct that can create competitive advantage of e-retailers for "external positioning vis-à-vis consumers and competitors, as well as for internal communication and orientation vis-à-vis employees" (ASEAN Secretariat 2020b, p. 8).

The World Economic Forum (2019) explained that industry self-regulation has gained its popularity and importance in the online market place because the current regulatory frameworks cannot address all issues associated with e-consumer protection. For instance, the International Organization for Standardization (ISO) (2013) first published ISO 10008:2013 specific for B2C e-commerce in 2013. This document provides guidelines to organizations to plan, design, develop, execute, maintain, and improve "an effective and efficient system concerning" B2B transactions (ISO 2013). The World Economic Forum (2019) also proposes that industry associations should work closely with other groups of stakeholders, such as consumer associations, to promote e-consumer protection.

Some good examples of a self-regulatory approach are (i) the codes of ethics and conduct of the Direct Selling Association of Singapore, (ii) the code of practice of Singapore Retailers Association, (iii) a set of regulation of Vietnam E-Commerce Association, and (iv) the code of ethics of the Internet and Mobile Marketing Association of the Philippines.

The Direct Selling Association of Singapore (2017) has a code of ethics that specifically stipulates the conduct for the protection of consumers, including clear guidelines on prohibited practices, and what businesses should and should not do in terms of "cooling-off and returning of goods, respect of privacy, fairness, referral selling and delivery" (pp. 6–7). The code of practice by Singapore Retailers Association (2020) advises members not to engage in unfair practices and to comply with relevant laws and regulations relating to consumer protection. The Internet and Mobile Marketing Code of Ethics, introduced by the Internet and Mobile Marketing Association of the Philippines in 2008, serves as a self-regulatory framework for members to observe ad comply with. It advises its members not to engage in false, deceptive, or misleading advertisement as these are prohibited under the *RA 7394 Consumer Act* of the Philippines (Toral 2008). This has great implications on consumer protection in both online and offline transactions. Vietnam E-Commerce Association (2015) is a nonprofit organization established in 2007 with corporate and individual members. Its main function is to support and protect its members' interest and contribute to the development of e-commerce in Vietnam. It advises its members to observe the e-commerce legal framework when involving in online transactions. It also assists its members to address conflicts relating to e-retailing business through negotiation, reconciliation, and mediation (Vietnam E-Commerce Association 2015).

Similar to guidelines, these codes are advisory, not mandatory. It should be noted that not all members of these associations subscribe such codes, and the effectiveness of these codes depends strongly on compliance measures and the back-up of regulation, that is, industry codes of practice can only work well with the support of government regulation and enforcement (Stöber, Kotzian and Weißenberger 2019).

However, some industry associations in the region do not introduce any codes of practice or such codes are not available to the public, and their main focus is to protect the interest of their members. For example, Indonesian E-Commerce Association (idEA) (2016), established in 2012 with nine founding e-commerce enterprises, aims to create a safe and conducive online marketplace by educating the public, working with stakeholders, including government and e-retailers. It also provides feedback to government pertaining to regulations that impact the industry (Indonesian E-Commerce Association 2016).

The Internet Alliance (undated) in Malaysia, an industry association with members that are Internet service providers, aims to provide information and services to its members and represents the industry to protect its members' interest by working with the government and stakeholders. It is the local Trust Partner of Ecommerce Foundation (a global e-commerce association), which awards the trust mark to web shops in Malaysia that meet the criteria of the Internet Alliance (undated).

Lao ICT Commerce Association (2020), established in 2005 by leading ICT companies in Vientiane, aims to develop strong collaboration among ICT-related businesses and educational institutions. Yet, very limited information about this association is available on its website.

Self-Regulation by E-Retailing

Within the market place, there is a shift from regulation to self-regulation and/or coregulation. Self-regulation refers to the minimum intervention or no intervention from government (Curtis 2005a). According to Berleur and Poullet (2006) and Cowles (2001b), self-regulation refers to voluntary norms and/or rules which are self-developed and accepted by the involved parties. Self-regulation may also include rules for good corporate governance, standards, and internal complaint-handling procedures (Taskforce on Industry Self-regulation 2000). E-retailers can build trust with customers and enhance their reputation by adopting self-regulation.

A number of initiatives and programs have been adopted by e-retailers to address online security and privacy issues. Most of the e-retailers have employed advanced technology applications, data analytics, and artificial intelligence to provide secure payment mechanisms. Examples of how e-retailers have protected their consumers online will be discussed in Chapter 4.

However, there has been insufficient effort to implement technological applications for privacy and security compliance and enforcement. This is evidenced by several cases of online security breach. For instance, personal information of 900,000 and 45,000 customers of Philippines Cebuana and True Corp (Thailand) were revealed by a marketing server breach in 2019 and 2018, respectively (Interpol Global Complex for Innovation 2020). The online shopping site Tokopedia in Indonesia experienced the worst personal data theft of 91 million accounts in 2020 (Hutton 2020). After this incident, Tokopedia's rank dropped from 25th place to 110th place in the list of most visited site in Indonesia (Hutton 2020). Given Tokopedia is one of the popular e-retailers in Indonesia, it suggests that self-regulatory mechanisms dealing with online incidents seem "haphazard" in many countries (OECD 2003c, p. 15).

Activities by Civil Society Organizations

According to the World Bank (cited in the World Economic Forum 2013), civil society generally includes nongovernmental organizations, nonprofit organizations, community and indigenous groups, charitable organizations, religious organizations, and professional associations and foundations (education, culture, environment, etc.). Such organizations are usually collectively owned by their members and aim to address social problems and increase societal benefits, for example, by improving social cohesion, alleviating poverty, promoting the interests of members (including the minority and marginalized groups), and protecting the environment (Jezard 2018). For instance, Consumers International is a nonprofit organization, and thus it can be considered as a part in the civil society ecosystem. The same applies to other consumer groups.

Activities by Consumer Associations

Consumer associations in different countries have advocated e-consumer rights, educated e-consumers, and provided guidance to e-consumers to seek redress. Internationally, there have been a number of alternative dispute resolution services provided by consumer association. For example, CHOICE, a consumer advocacy group in Australia, provides information and advice that is "free from commercial bias" (CHOICE 2020, para. 1). In the early days, in the 1970s, it was involved in the drafting of the Australia's *Trade Practices Act*. Later, it also advocated for the enactment of the *Australian Consumer Law*, which legalize consumer rights (CHOICE 2020).

The International Consumer Protection and Enforcement Network (ICPEN), established in 1992, is a membership organization with members who are consumer protection law enforcement authorities from 64 countries (ICPEN 2020a). This network encourages members to share best practice and information on consumer protection issues and new trends and collaborate to enhance consumer protection enforcement (ICPEN, 2020b). ICPEN's work has great impact on consumers' interests and foster global cooperation among law enforcement authorities (World Economic Forum 2019).

Similar to the ICPEN, Consumers International is a membership organization with more than 200 members that are consumer advocacy groups in more than 100 countries (Consumers International 2020a). As pointed out by the World Economic Forum (2019), the current regulatory framework for e-consumer protection cannot keep pace with the rapid development of the online market; and, thus activities and initiatives pertaining to e-consumer protection by the third sector would complement the governance framework for e-consumer protections. The main functions of Consumers International are to promote consumer rights, justice, and protection and represent consumers' voice at the international level (Consumers International 2020b).

Regionally, the South East Asian Consumers Council (SEACC), a consumer organization, consists of consumer associations in ASEAN state members. Its main function is to safeguard the interests of consumers, empower consumers in the region, and collaborate with civil society at various levels (national, regional, and international) to promote consumers' interests (South East Asian Consumers Council 2020).

At the national level, most ASEAN countries have at least one consumer organization or association. Most of these organizations are not-for-profit and nongovernmental, and their main functions is to advance consumers' interest via providing information, educating consumers, and advocating policy and regulations for better consumer protection (Consumers Association of Singapore undated b). The list of consumer associations in ASEAN countries that are relevant to e-consumer protection is exhibited in Table 3.5.

Table 3.5 Consumer associations in ASEAN countries

Country	Consumer association
Brunei Darussalam	✓ Consumer Association of Brunei Darussalam (CAB)
Cambodia	✓ Cambodian Consumer Association (CCASSO)
Indonesia	✓ Indonesian Consumers Organization (YLKI)
Laos People's Democratic Republic (Laos)	✓ Lao ICT Commerce Association (LACI)
Malaysia	✓ Federation of Malaysian Consumers Associations (FOMCA) ✓ Consumers Association of Penang (CAP) ✓ Malaysian Consumers Protection Association (PPPM) ✓ National Consumer Complaints Centre ✓ Malaysian Association of Standards Users
Myanmar	✓ Myanmar Consumer Union
Philippines	✓ IBON Foundation
Singapore	✓ Consumers Association of Singapore (CASE)
Thailand	✓ Foundation for Consumers (FFC)
Vietnam	✓ Vietnam Standard & Consumer Association (VINASTAS)

Source: Compiled from South East Asian Consumers Council (2020), Federation of Malaysian Consumers Associations (FOMCA) (2015), Consumers Association of Singapore (CASE) (undated b), Consumers International (2011), ASEAN Secretariat (2018)

Conclusion

This chapter discusses the regulatory and nonregulatory policy frameworks for consumer protection at the national, regional, and international levels. A number of principles, guidelines, and legislation have been introduced by the UN, the EU, the OECD, the APEC, and ASEAN to enhance e-consumer protection and facilitate the development of e-retailing. Yet, such guidelines are advisory, and not mandatory, with unclear mechanisms to enforce them. Both the UN and the OECD Guidelines promote voluntary adoption and compliance with international guidelines and principles. These guidelines complement existing national legal frameworks for e-consumer protection rather than replace them. The level of compliance may vary among organizations and countries, depending on several factors.

Internationally, there are a number of guidelines to provide directions to countries. However, there has been no measure for international organizations to deal with member countries which do not comply with these guidelines. Furthermore, nonuniform regulations and standards in different countries have made e-consumer protection more difficult and challenging due to ambiguous jurisdiction applications and difficulties in enforcement. Yet, different countries can adopt these international guidelines to review and develop their current policies on e-consumer protection (Harland 1999).

Given the fast developing state of e-retailing, its special features, and an increase in the number of issues associated with online shopping, e-retailing requires a different legal and technological approach to fully develop its potential (Office of Communications (UK) 2006). Also, it is observed that the laws of many countries have been enacted over a decade ago and many have not been revised since that time. Yet, e-retailing has grown significantly in the last decade. Thus, it is necessary to revise the fundamental ground rules to smooth the progress of global e-retailing. Nevertheless, too much regulation would burden e-retailers and could prevent the growth of e-retailing. On the other hand, e-retailing without government intervention may become a platform for potential fraud and misdeeds. Thus, a governance framework embracing these two regulatory and nonregulatory measures to protect e-consumers will be examined in the next chapter.

References

APEC. 1998. *APEC Blueprint for Action on Electronic Commerce*. Singapore: APEC. https://www.apec.org/Meeting-Papers/Leaders-Declarations/1998/1998_aelm/apec_blueprint_for.aspx

APEC. 2002. *Voluntary Online Consumer Protection Guidelines*. www.export.gov/apececommerce/cp/guidelines.htm.

APEC. 2017. *APEC Internet and Digital Economy Roadmap*. Danang: APEC.

APEC. undated. *ANNEX A: APEC Cross-Border E-Commerce Facilitation Framework*. Singapore: APEC.

APEC Electronic Commerce Steering Group. 2007. *Development of "APEC Guidance for Electronic Commerce", Using the Best Practices of E-government Procurement Systems*. Singapore: APEC Secretariat.

APEC Electric Commerce Steering Group. 2020. *Regulations, Policies and Initiatives on E-Commerce and Digital Economy for APEC MSMEs' Participation in the Region*. Singapore: APEC.

ASEAN Secretariat. 2012. *e-ASEAN Framework Agreement*. Jakarta: ASEAN. https://asean.org/?static_post=e-asean-framework-agreement

ASEAN Secretariat. 2017. *Master Plan on ASEAN Connectivity 2025*. Jakarta: ASEAN.

ASEAN Secretariat. 2018. *Handbook on ASEAN Consumer Protection Laws and Regulation*. Jakarta: ASEAN Secretariat.

ASEAN Secretariat. 2020a. *Thailand. Jakarta: ASEAN Secretariat*. https://aseanconsumer.org/selectcountry=Thailand

ASEAN Secretariat. 2020b. ASEAN Online Business Code of Conduct. Jakarta: ASEAN Secretariat.

ASOCIO Secretariat Office. 2017. *Lao ICT Commerce Association*. Association. Petailing Jaya: ASOCIO Secretariat Office.

Ayub, Z.A., Z.M. Yusoff, and N.A. Sharif. 2007. *"Malaysian Electronic Commerce Act 2006 and EU directives: Consumer protection perspectives." Journal of Ethics, Legal and Governance* 3. pp. 68–76.

Balfas, H.M. 2009. "The Indonesian Law on Electronic Information and Transactions." *Digital Evidence and Electronic Signature Law Review* 6, pp. 202–206.

Bangko Sentral ng Pilipinas. undated. *Circular No. 542 Series of 2006*. Manila: Bangko Sentral ng Pilipinas.

Bangkok Post. 2019. The reach and liabilities of the Personal Data Protection Act. *Bangkok Post*, September 3, 2019. https://bangkokpost.com/business/1741919/the-reach-and-liabilities-of-the-personal-data-protection-act

Cauffman, C. 2019. "New EU rules on business-to-consumer and platform-to-business relationships." *Maastricht Journal of European and Comparative Law* 264, pp. 469–479. doi:10.1177/1023263X19865835

Chanpanich, T., and G. Mahakunkitchareon. 2019. *Thailand's Legal System Undergoes Major Digital Reforms*. Bangkok: Tilleke & Gibbins International Ltd.

Chandran, R. 2004. "Consumer Protection (Fair Trading) Act." *Singapore Journal of Legal Studies* July 2004, pp. 192–226.

CHOICE. 2020. *The CHOICE Story*. Marrickville, NSW: CHOICE. https://www.choice.com.au/about-us/the-choice-story

Consumers Association of Singapore (CASE). undated a. *CPFTA & Lemon Law*. Singapore: CASE.

Consumers Association of Singapore (CASE). undated b. *Introduction*. Singapore: CASE.

Consumers International. 2020a. *Who we are*. London: Consumers International. https://consumersinternational.org/who-we-are/

Consumers International. 2020b. *What we do*. London: Consumers International. https://consumersinternational.org/what-we-do/

Consumers International. 2011. *Roadmapping Capacity Building Needs In Consumer Protection In ASEAN: Country Report: The Kingdom Of Cambodia (Final)*. Jakarta: ASEAN (AADCP II).

Cornelius, K. 2006. *Chapter 1: International Legal Instruments*. In *European Cybercrime Law*. Saarbrücken: Institut fur Rechtsinformatik.

Cruz, G.D. 2018. *Privacy and Data Protection Laws in Southeast Asia*. Quezon city: Ateneo de Manila University. http://ateneo.edu/udpo/article/Privacy-and-data-protection-laws-southeast-asia

Department of Economic Planning and Development (Brunei Darussalam). undated. *Our Law - Consumer Protection*. Bandar Seri Begawan: Ministry of Finance and Economy (Brunei Darussalam).

Department of Information and Communications Technology (Philippines). undated. *Cybercrime Investigation and Coordinating Center (CICC)*. Department of Information and Communications Technology (Philippines). https://dict.gov.ph/cybercrime-investigation-and-coordinating-center-cicc/

Department of Trade and Industry undated. Consumer Protection Online. Metro Manila: Department of Trade and Industry, Philippines. https://dti.gov.ph/negosyo/e-commerce/consumer-protection-online/

Direct Selling Association of Singapore. 2017. Direct Selling Code of Ethics. Singapore: Direct Selling Association of Singapore.

Dunn, M. 2005. *A Comparative Analysis of Cybersecurity Initiatives Worldwide*. In *WSIS Thematic Meeting on Cybersecurity, 28 June1 July 2005*. Geneva: International Telecommunication Union.

ecInsider. 2014. *Understanding E-Commerce Legislation in Malaysia*. https://ecinsider.my/2014/07/understanding-ecommerce-legislation-malaysia.html

Federation of Malaysian Consumers Associations (FOMCA). 2015. *Worldwide Consumer Association. Johor Bahru: Federation of Malaysian Consumers Associations*.

Ha, H. 2011. "Security and Privacy in E-consumer Protection in Victoria, Australia." 5th *International Conference on Trust Management* (TM), 240252. June 2011, Copenhagen, Denmark.

Ha, H. 2012. "Online Security and Consumer Protection in E-commerce - An Australian case." In *Strategic and Pragmatic E-Business: Implications for Future Business Practices,* ed. K.M. Rezaul, 217–243. Hershey, PA: IGI Global.

Ha, H. 2017. "Stakeholders' Views on Self-Regulation to Protect Consumers in E-Retailing." *Journal of Electronic Commerce in Organizations* 15, no. 3, pp. 83–103

Ha, H., and K. Coghill. 2008. "Online shoppers in Australia: dealing with problems." *International Journal of Consumer Studies* 32, no. 1, pp. 5–17.

Ha, H., K. Coghill, and E.A. Maharaj. 2009. "Current Measures to Protect E-consumers' Privacy in Australia". In Chen, K. and Fadlalla, A. *Online Consumer Protection: Theories of Human Relativism,* 123–150. Hershey, PA: Idea Group, Inc.

Harland, D. "The United Nations Guidelines for Consumer Protection." *Journal of Consumer Policy* 10, no. 2, pp. 245–266.

Heseltine, C. 2007. *APEC - Meeting the Challenges of Regional E-Commerce.* APEC. https://apec.org/Press/Blogs/2007/1109_jpn_ambhaseltinegbde

Hutton, J. 2020. "Indonesia Beefs Up Cyber Security After Data Breaches." *The Straits Times,* July 12, 2020.

ICPEN (International Consumer Protection and Enforcement Network). 2020a. *Who we are.* ICPEN. https://icpen.org/who-we-are

ICPEN (International Consumer Protection and Enforcement Network). 2020b. *What we do.* ICPEN. From https://icpen.org/what-we-do

Indonesian E-Commerce Association. 2016. About us. Jakarta: Indonesian E-Commerce Association.

Internet Alliance. undated. Shop.Safe. Kuala Lumpur: Internet Alliance. https:// internetalliance.my/safe-shop/

Interpol Global Complex for Innovation. 2020. ASEAN Cyberthreat Assessment 2020: Key *Insights from the ASEAN Cybercrime Operations Desk.* Singapore: Interpol Global Complex for Innovation.

ISO (the International Organization for Standardization) 2013. *ISO 10008:2013(en) Quality management - Customer satisfaction - Guidelines for business-to-consumer electronic commerce transactions.* Geneva: ISO.

ITU. 2020. *UN Resolutions Related to Cybersecurity.* https://www.itu.int/en/ action/ cybersecurity/Pages/un-resolutions.aspx

Jezard, A. 2018. *Who and what is 'civil society?'.* Geneva: World Economic Forum. https://weforum.org/agenda/2018/04/what-is-civil-society/

Johnson, C. 2014. *Burma: Consumer Protection Law Adopted.* Washington, DC: The Library of Congress.

Kiratisountorn, T., P. Eianleng, A. Gamvros, and R. Kwok. 2020. *Thailand Personal Data Protection Law*. Norton Rose Fulbright Data LLP. https://dataprotectionreport.com/2020/02/thailand-personal-data-protection-law/

KPMG Cambodia Ltd. 2019. *Technical Update*. Phnom Penh: KPMG Cambodia Ltd.

Kyaw, H.M. 2014. "Burma President Approves Consumer Protection Law." *The Irrawaddy* March 17, 2014.

Lao ICT Commerce Association (LICA). 2020. Association Overview. Vientiane: Lao ICT Commerce Association (LICA). https://lica.la/association-overview/

Lau, K.H. 2017. "A Guide to Singapore's Lemon Law – The law protecting consumers in Singapore." *Asia Law Network*. https://learn.asialawnetwork.com/2017/12/05/a-guide-to-singapores-lemon-law-the-law-protecting-consumers-in-singapore/

Le, T.V. 2019. *Data Protection in Vietnam: Overview*. Thomson Reuters. https://amchamvietnam.com/wp-content/uploads/2019/05/Data-Protection-in-Vietnam-Overview-April-2019.pdf

Malaysian Communications and Multimedia Commission. 2020. *Digital Signature*. Selangor Darul Ehsan: Malaysian Communications and Multimedia Commission.

Malaysia Ministry of Domestic Trade and Consumer Affairs 2020. *Consumer Advisory Council. Wilayah Persekutuan*. Putrajaya: Malaysia Ministry of Domestic Trade and Consumer Affairs.

Medina, A.F. 2020. *Indonesia's law on E-Commerce: Clear Guidelines and Compliance by November 2021*. ASEAN briefing. https://aseanbriefing.com/news/indonesias-law-on-e-commerce-clear-guidelines-and-compliance-by-november-2021/

Mendiola, J. 2019. *Thailand Facilitates Key Digital Reforms Through Electronic Transaction Act Amendments*. Bangkok: Silk Legal Co. Ltd. https://silklegal.com/thailand-facilitates/

Mendoza, J.P., Dekker, H.C., and J.L. Wielhouwer. 2020. "Industry Self-regulation Under Government Intervention." *Journal of Quantitative Criminology* 36, pp. 183–205. doi: 10.1007/s10940-019-09424-x

Ministry of Industry and Trade, Vietnam Competition and Consumer Authority. 2019. *Annual Report 2019*. Hanoi, Ministry of Industry and Trade, Vietnam Competition and Consumer Authority.

Ministry of Justice (Vietnam). 2018. *Passing the Law on cybersecurity*. Hanoi: Ministry of Justice (Vietnam). https://moj.gov.vn/en/Pages/Activities-of-public-administrative-and-justice-reform.aspx?Ite mID=3255

National Cyber Security Agency. 2020. *Computer Crimes Act 1997*. Putrajaya: National Cyber Security Agency.

National Privacy Commission (Philippines) undated. *Republic Act 10173 – Data Privacy Act of 2012*. Manila: National Privacy Commission (Philippines). https://privacy.gov.ph/quickguide/

Nethin, J. 2010. "A Comparative Study of Problems in Consumer Protection Laws for Electronic Commerce (E-Commerce) in Thailand and the United States." *Thailand Law Journal 13*, no. 1. Online. http://thailawforum.com/articles/comparative-study-of-problem.html

OECD. 2000a. *Reducing the Risk of Policy Failure: Challenges for Regulatory Compliance*. Paris: OECD.

OECD. 2000b. *Guidelines for Consumer Protection in the Context of Electronic Commerce*. Paris: OECD.

OECD. 2002b. *Report on Consumer Protections for Payment Cardholders*. Paris: OECD.

OECD. 2003b. *Implementation Plan for the OECD Guidelines for the Security of Information Systems and Networks: towards a Culture of Security*. Paris: OECD.

OECD. 2006. *Consumer Dispute Resolution and Redress in the Global Marketplace*. Paris: OECD.

OECD. 2007. *OECD Recommendation on Consumer Dispute Resolution and Redress*. Paris: OECD.

OECD. 2013. *OECD Privacy Framework*. Paris: OECD.

OECD. 2015. *Digital Security Risk Management for Economic and Social Prosperity: OECD Recommendation and Companion Document*. OECD Publishing, Paris. doi: 10.1787/9789264245471-en

OECD. 2016. *Consumer Protection in E-commerce: OECD Recommendation*. Paris: OECD Publishing. doi: 10.1787/9789264255258-en

OECD. 2018. *Consumer Protection Enforcement in a Global Digital Marketplace*. OECD Digital Economy Papers March 2018, no. 266. Paris: OECD.

OECD. 2019. *Challenges to Consumer Policy in The Digital Age*. Paris: OECD.

Personal Data Protection Commission. undated. *PDPA Overview*. Singapore: Personal Data Protection Commission.

Proton Technologies AG. 2020. *What is GDPR, the EU's new data protection law?* Proton Technologies AG. https://gdpr.eu/what-is-gdpr/

Qaqaya, H. 2012. "Ad Hoc Expert Meeting on the Interface between Competition and Consumer Policies." July 12, 2012 Geneva, Palais des Nations. Geneva: UNCTAD. https://unctad.org/meetings/en/Presentation/ciclp2012_Opening_Qaqaya_en.pdf

Rohendi, A. 2015. "Consumer Protection in the E-Commerce: Indonesian Law and International Law Perspective (September 22, 2015)." *Ecodemica* III, no. 2, pp. 478–488. https://ssrn.com/abstract= 2678754 or http://dx.doi.org/10.2139/ssrn.2678754

Salazar, L.C. 2007. *Getting a Dial Tone: Telecommunications Liberalization in Malaysia and the Philippines*. Singapore: Institute of Southeast Asian Studies (ISEAS).

Sathye, M., E. Clark, E., and A. Dugdale. 2004. *Fraud in E-government Transactions: Risks and Remedies*. Discussion Paper No. 14. Parkes, ACT Australian Government Information Management Office.

Sengpunya, P. 2019. "ASEAN E-Commerce Legal Framework and Alignment of Lao PDR: A Review." Lentera Hukum 6, no. 3, pp. 369–390.

Singapore Retailers Association. 2020. *Code of practice*. Singapore: Singapore Retailers Association

South East Asian Consumers Council (SEACC). 2020. *Who we are*. Jakarta: South East Asian Consumers Council (SEACC).

Stöber, T., P. Kotzian, and B.E. Weißenberger. 2019. "Design matters: on the Impact of Compliance Program Design on Corporate Ethics." *Business Research* 12, pp. 383–424.

Tanodomdej, P. 2017. *E-Consumer Protection in ASEAN at the Crossroads: Challenges in the Harmonization of E-Commerce Law*. Bangkok: German-Southeast Asian Center of Excellence for Public Policy and Good Governance (CPG).

Thailand Law Forum. 2009. *Consumer protection Act, B.E. 2522 1979*. Thailand Law Forum. http://thailawforum.com/database1/ConsumerProtecting-law.html

The Authority for Info-communications Technology Industry (Brunei). 2018. *Content Regulation*. Jalan Berakas: The Authority for Info-communications Technology Industry (Brunei). https://aiti.gov.bn/SitePages/Content-Regulation.aspx

The Jakarta Post. 2019. "Seven Things You Need to Know About the New E-Commerce Regulation." *The Jakarta Post*, December 12, 2019. https://www.thejakartapost.com/news/2019/12/12/seven-things-you-need-to-know-about-the-new-e-commerce-regulation.html

The Star Online. 2020. "Vietnam Government Drafts Decree to Protect Personal Data." *The Star Online*, January 24, 2020. https://thestar.com.my/news/regional/2020/01/14/vietnam-government-drafts-decree-to-protect-personal-data

Tilleke and Gibbins. 2019. *Cambodia Enacts a New E-commerce Law and a Consumer Protection Law*. Phnom Penh: Tilleke and Gibbins.

Toral, J. 2008. "Internet and Mobile Advertising Code of Ethics." GMA News Online, September 16, 2008. https://gmanetwork.com/news/opinion/content/120724/internet-and-mobile-advertising-code-of-ethics/story/

Trend Micro. 2019. *EU General Data Protection Regulation (GDPR)*. Trend Micro. https://trendmicro.com/vinfo/in/security/definition/eu-general-data-protection-regulation-gdpr

Urbas, G. 2008. *An Overview of Cybercrime Legislation and Cases in Singapore.* Working Paper Series No. 001. Singapore: Asian Law Institute.

UNCTAD. undated. *Online Consumer Protection Legislation Worldwide.* Geneva: UNCTAD. https://unctad.org/en/Pages/DTL/STI_and_ICTs/ICT4D-Legislation/eCom-Consumer-Protection-Laws.aspx (accessed on July 12, 2020).

UNCTAD. 2013. *Review of E-Commerce Legislation Harmonization in the Association of Southeast Asian Nations.* Geneva: UNCTAD.

UNCTAD. 2017. *Consumer Protection in Electronic Commerce.* Geneva: UNCTAD.

World Economic Forum 2019. *The Global Governance of Online Consumer Protection and E-Commerce Building Trust.* Geneva: World Economic Forum.

UNCTAD. 2018a. *Manual on consumer protection.* Geneva: UNCTAD.

UNCTAD 2018b. *Lao People's Democratic Republic Rapid eTrade Readiness Assessment.* Geneva: UNCTAD.

UNCTAD. 2019. *Voluntary peer review of the consumer protection law and policy of Indonesia: Overview.* Geneva: UNCTAD.

United Nations. 2010. *Resolution Adopted by the General Assembly on 21 December 2009 64/211. Creation of a Global Culture of Cybersecurity and Taking Stock of National Efforts to Protect Critical Information Infrastructures.* New York, NY: United Nations.

United Nations. 2014. *Resolution adopted by the General Assembly on 18 December 2013: 68/167. The right to privacy in the digital age.* New York, NY: United Nations.

United Nations. 2016. *United Nations guidelines for consumer protection. (UNCTAD/DITC/CPLP/ MISC/ 2016/1).* New York and Geneva: United Nations Conference on Trade and Development.

Vietnam E-Commerce Association. 2015. *Regulations.* Hanoi: Vietnam E-Commerce Association.

World Economic Forum. 2013. *The Future Role of Civil Society.* Geneva: World Economic Forum, and KPMG International.

World Economic Forum. 2019. *The Global Governance of Online Consumer Protection and E-commerce Building Trust.* Geneva: World Economic Forum.

CHAPTER 4

A Proposed Multisector Governance Framework for E-Consumer Protection

Introduction

In the digital economy, governance has to respond to rapid information technology, socioeconomic, and political changes caused by globalization. Thus, this chapter examines governance in the context of e-retailing to consider issues which do not exist or which do exist in different forms in traditional commerce, such as online security and privacy incidents. Importantly, it explains the limitations of the current three-section governance framework for e-consumer protection and proposes a four-sector governance framework that can apply to e-retailing in order to enhance protection to e-consumers. This chapter discusses the concepts of public governance ("governance") and global governance, the principles of good governance, in general. It explains the complexity of a governance system. In doing so, this study focuses on participation by all stakeholders, including e-consumers, as an element of good and democratic governance.

This chapter consists of three main sections, followed by the conclusion. The first section discusses the concept of governance, and principles of good governance, in general, and in the context of e-retailing. In the second section, the current three-sector governance framework for e-consumer protection is elaborated. The third section proposes a four-sector governance framework to enhance the protection of e-consumers in e-retailing, including the active involvement of e-consumers as the fourth sector.

Governance

Concept of Governance

There is no single definition of governance as it has been defined by different authors and organizations and from different aspects. The United Nations Development Program (UNDP) (1997) defines governance as

> the exercise of economic, political and administrative authority to manage a country's affairs at all levels. It comprises mechanisms, processes and institutions through which citizens and groups articulate their interests, exercise their legal rights, meet their obligations and mediate their differences. (p. 10)

Pyone, Smith and van den Broek (2019) defined governance as

> the rules (both formal and informal) for collective action and decision making in a system with diverse players and organizations while no formal control mechanism can dictate the relationship among those players and organizations. (p. 710)

The IMF (2020) elaborates that

> governance is a broad concept covering all aspects of how a country is governed, including its economic policies, regulatory framework, and adherence to rule of law. (para. 1)

According to the Governance Institute of Australia (2020), governance is

> Governance encompasses the system by which an organization is controlled and operates, and the mechanisms by which it, and its people, are held to account. Ethics, risk management, compliance and administration are all elements of governance. (para. 1)

These definitions infer that governance embraces the following main components:

1. The exercise of economic, social, and political power and authority to manage resources and affairs of a country (or an organization) for

a specific objective, for example, achieving socioeconomic, political/ legal, or environmental goals;

2. Institutions, mechanisms, processes, convention, and specific actions which affect the way such power and authority is exercised; and

3. The manner in which individuals, groups, and organizations, the public and private sectors and civil society, the ruler and the ruled, and formal and informal institutions interact with one another to provide resolutions for conflict among different groups of stake-holders due to their diverse interests.

In addition, Kooiman (1999), Rhodes (1996), and Stocker (1998) view governance as interactive networks, including processes which could solve societal problems. Kooiman (1999) explained that governance embraces the three spheres of governance, that is, government (the state or the public sector), business (the market or the private sector), and civil society (the third sector or civil society organizations [CSOs]). It includes

all those interactive arrangement in which public as well as private actors participate aimed at solving societal problems or creating societal opportunities and attending to the institutions within which these governing activities take place. (Kooiman 1999, p. 70)

Weiss (2001), Ha (2011, 2017), and Shergold (2016) also noted that the three spheres of governance, including the state (government), the private sector, and CSOs, were interrelated and interdependent. Kaufmann, Kraay and Mastruzzi (2008) emphasized the key dimensions of governance, namely "voice and accountability, political stability and absence of violence/terrorism, government effectiveness, regulatory quality, rule of law, and control of corruption" (p. 1). Therefore, governance must embrace not only mechanisms and processes, but also the relationships and institutions through which different spheres of governance perform their duty and exercise their rights (UNDP 1997).

No matter from what dimension or aspects of governance is examined, governance is complex and comprises several sectors, several courses of action, and covers all areas, namely social, legal, political, economic, environmental, and technological. These concepts and definitions are the groundwork for the development of an integrated governance framework for e-consumer protection discussed next.

Governance of E-Retailing

Apart from its anonymous and transient nature, e-retailers adopt advanced technology to disseminate information and exchange communication online at a rapid speed in order to respond to a greater demand for a wider range of e-services and products, especially during the recent COVID-19 pandemic (World Trade Organization 2020). The Internet becomes an online platform for market exchanges to occur between buyers and sellers (Duch-Brown 2017). The operations of the e-market make political jurisdictions more complex since "connection costs are insensitive to distance and political boundaries"(Mathiason et al. 2004, p. 7). These special features of the e-market make the governance of e-retailing significantly different from the governance of traditional commerce because the adoption of new technology, including digital disruptive innovation, by e-retailers has blurred the geographical boundaries of the online markets that makes it tougher to determine legal jurisdictions (Atluri, Dietz and Henke 2017). Hence, the definition of governance has to take into consideration the special features of e-retailing.

Since governance of e-retailing does not entirely rely on any existing forms of government structure, and given its unique characteristics, this study combines and modifies various definitions of governance to develop a definition of governance in e-retailing. Specifically, the inclusion of all groups of stakeholders has enriched the concept of governance. Thus, for the purpose of this study, governance of e-retailing is defined as

> a complex system of institutions, structures, mechanisms, functions, and processes characterized by the interaction among government, e-retailers, civil society organizations in the management of resources to establish agreements about standards, policies, rules, and enforcement mechanisms and dispute resolution procedures to apply to global internetworking activities in e-retailing in order to achieve socio-economic and political objectives.

In this study, institutions include different government agencies, CSOs, and business entities. Structures refer to the operation of these organizations at the international, regional, and national levels. Mechanisms consist of regulation and self-regulation (Braithwaite and Drahos 2000; OECD 2015). As highlighted by the OECD (2018b) and Nooren et al. (2018), the development and adoption of e-platforms for commercial transactions has put pressure on existing government regulation for facilitating innovation and economic development as well as for protecting public interests. The pressure on excessive government regulations or the absence of such regulations encourage industries and businesses to self-regulate to reduce compliance costs, reduce various types of risks to consumers, enhance public trust, and prevent or combat negative public perceptions of their operations (Castro 2011). The main mechanisms for self-regulation of e-retailing are corporate governance and corporate social responsibility (CSR) (Albareda 2008; OECD 2015; Sahut et al. 2019). Functions and processes refer to various roles and activities of different groups of stakeholders. Economic, social, and political objectives refer to the growth of e-retailing, the improvement of consumer trust and confidence, and the enhancement of democracy and public acceptability, respectively. However, this volume will focus on the stakeholders and their roles.

Governance System

According to the definition of e-retailing governance, a governance system reflects complex relationships among political (the state or government or the public sector), economic (the private sector or business or e-retailers), and societal sectors (CSOs or the third sector). The complex governance system not only includes the state governed by political institutions, but also transcends the state by embracing nonstate sectors (Breslin and Nesadurai 2018; *World Economic Forum 2019*). Nonstate sectors include two main groups: market/business (e-retailers) and CSOs (including industry and consumer associations).

The existing regulatory frameworks may not be robust enough to govern new business frameworks, adopting new and/or disruptive technologies, in the online marketplace (Productivity Commission (Australia)

2016). However, government still plays the main role in this complex system. Government will obtain and deploy its power in new areas as well as take on a new role in governing the private sector's conduct—for example, introducing new ways to guide business and individuals on their responsibility of managing data in the digital age (Jarrar 2017; Kourula et al. 2019). Yet, government's responsibility and functions are shared with the other two sectors, and it also needs to embrace change, openness, and partnerships.

Market forces and new technology are considered the fundamental drivers for competition among e-retailers (The Nielsen Company (United States), LLC. 2018). However, online businesses consist of several types of e-retailers which do not share uniform values, objectives, or practices, and thus some forms of soft regulation are essential (OECD 2015). The imbalance of power among e-consumers and e-retailers, regarding the anonymity of e-retailers and different business practices, may lead to market failure which justifies government intervention (Jarrar 2017; Kourula et al. 2019). CSOs also need to provide support to e-retailers as "the benefits for civil society of working more closely with business are clear" (Sriskandarajah 2017, para. 1). First, e-retailers have faced persistent and rigorous pressure to remain competitive and profitable given the rapid development of globalization. Second, e-retailers have to handle both the current problems occurring in traditional commerce and newly arising problems in the online market, to meet the expectations of different groups of stakeholders. Yet, e-retailers are unable to address all these challenges alone. Therefore, government could provide the right conditions for e-retailers to operate, whereas CSOs could provide e-retailers with information and feedback, and educate e-consumers (OECD 2009; *World Economic Forum 2019*). CSOs balance the governance system. Without CSOs the system will be imbalanced. As Sacks (1996) has argued:

> (w)ithout a strong civil society, even political and economic structures [would] fail. (p. 17)

Although government cannot be totally replaced, government needs inputs from other sectors to fulfill its roles (Butcher and Gilchris 2016) Together with business, CSOs have increasingly played an important role in supplementing the public sector (state) to ensure a higher level of democracy and participation (Nalinakumari and MacLean 2005).

Sadowsky, Zambrano and Dandjinou (2004) highlighted that these two sectors could presume their responsibilities in governance on matters related to Internet governance. This can help government to maintain transparency, accountability, and effective provision of public services in order to meet the public expectation and serve the public interest. On the other hand, CSOs may be more effective if the environment in which they operate is enabling since CSOs need a "touchstone" or a "canvas" for their activities (Huetter 2002, p. 3).

Overall, government produces a favorable political and legal environment for the private sector and civil society to operate productively. A constructive interaction among all sectors will improve good governance which can, in turn, increase economic performance, encourage participation, and promote democracy in the digital age (The UN Secretary-General's High-level Panel on Digital Cooperation 2019). The interaction among these sectors is reflected through "political exchange" between government and the third sector; "regulatory exchange" between government and business; and "commercial exchange" between business and civil society (Midttun 2005, p. 3). Midttun (2005) emphasized that

> civil society [was] seen as articulator and carrier of norms and values, but also supplier of workforce and taxes. Industry [could] be seen as providers of goods and services, but also jobs and taxes. Finally, Government [could] be seen as the locus for legitimate political aggregation of collective interest, but also provide[d] of public service. (p. 2)

OECD (2013) further commented that when the three sectors of society effectively worked together, the governance outcomes would become better. On the contrary, without effective partnerships, all stakeholders would lose:

> ... business loses opportunity, government loses credibility but society loses most of all. (Gupta 2005, p. 1)

Lee (2019) asserts that it is important to build trust and enhancement, and collaboration among the three sectors at various levels in order to improve the current multistakeholder global cooperation architecture is the way forward. The basic question here is how much government intervention is needed and how much can be left to other sectors. This depends on several economic, political, cultural, social, technological, and environmental determinants. In many cases, government intervenes when there is market or system failure, structural rigidities, or anticipatory myopia (Salmenkaita and Salo 2002).[1] There is no absolute formula to decide on the appropriate amount of government intervention, or the participation by other sectors.

Principles of Good Governance and E-Retailing

The quality of governance affects the outcome of any governance framework. Good governance refers to the competency of government to manage

> a country's resources and affairs in a manner that is open, transparent, accountable, equitable and responsive to people's needs. (Australian Government's Overseas Aid Program (AusAID) 2000, p. 3)

The World Bank (2003) identifies six indicators of good governance, including accountability, rule of law, effectiveness, consultation (voice), and predictability (political stability), which are discussed in the next section.[2]

Good governance is reflected through the quality of government–citizen relationships and the processes which government adopts to fulfill its duties to its citizens (Coghill 2004b; OECD 2018b). Such quality has great impacts on investment and growth, and thus would stimulate economic growth, embracing the growth of e-retailing and addressing issues occurring in the online marketplace.

---

[1] Anticipatory myopia means "individuals and organizations may under-invest in the generation and assimilation of information that contributes to their ability to act with foresight" (Salmenkaita and Salo 2002, p. 184).

[2] The six measured indicators of good governance are voice and accountability, political stability and lack of violence, government effectiveness, regulatory quality, rule of law, and control of corruption (World Bank, 2003).

The principles of good governance presented in Figure 4.1 are derived from the definitions of good governance by the World Economic Forum, International Business Leaders Forum, and John. F. Kennedy School of Government (2005), the United Nations Economic and Social Commission for Asia and the Pacific (2005), the Commission of the European Communities (2001), the Asian Development Bank (2000), the World Conference on Governance (1999), and Bruce-Lockhart (2016). However, given their relevance to e-consumer protection, this study focuses on five principles, namely responsiveness, transparency and openness, participation/inclusion, consultation/consensus, and accountability.

The first principle of good governance is responsiveness. Government must be responsive (Principle 1 in this study) to the needs of e-consumers for more effective protection in the online marketplace.

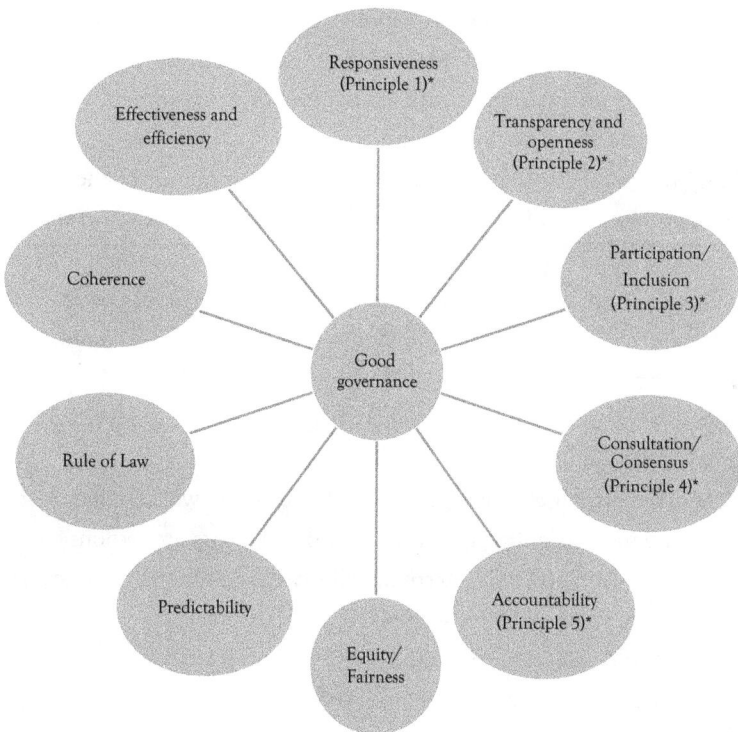

Figure 4.1 Main principles of good governance

*The five numbered principles are the five principles which are discussed in this study.

Transparency and openness (Principle 2) refers to the timely disclosure of relevant and accurate information about the activities of government and the provision of greater access to government documents (Fox 2007; OECD 2018b, 2019c). In e-retailing, information relating to new trends of online threats, and what government does to protect e-consumers, must be disseminated promptly and precisely to enhance public awareness and attract attention of the parties involved for timely solutions. This contributes to enhancing e-consumers' trust and confidence in e-retailing as they know that they can rely on government if something goes wrong.

Participation (Principle 3) calls for robust cooperation among all stakeholders to mobilize resources that are necessary for the development of e-retailing and for e-consumer protection. Wilson (2005) and the OECD (2018c) noted that it was the rights and responsibilities of different groups of stakeholders to participate effectively in the governance of e-retailing. Such participation can encourage greater representation and democratic governance. The participation principle enables all stakeholders to be included in the policy-making and implementation processes.

Good governance promotes consensus orientation (Principle 4) which ensures that policy-making decisions reflect the best interests of all affected parties and that public interest must prevail over the private one (United Nations Economic and Social Commission for Asia and the Pacific 2005). Consensus facilitates the establishment of clear and consistent regulations, and uniform and effective mechanisms of law enforcement across jurisdictions (Commission of the European Communities 2001). Consensus can be achieved by consultation (Principle 4) and discussions with e-consumers, e-retailers, and CSOs (Asian Development Bank (ADB) 2000).

Another attribute is accountability (Principle 5) which refers to the extent to which government officials and departments are responsible for their actions (Lam 2002/03). Accountability can similarly apply to e-retailers and CSOs that have to be accountable for their actions.

The World Economic Forum (2017) further explained that the concept of agile governance, apart from good governance, aims to modify the way that policies are formulated, debated, enacted, and enforced in the new industrial revolution. It is expected that governance should be more responsive or "agile to keep pace with the rapid changes of society—driven significantly by the rapid development and deployment of emerging technologies" (World Economic Forum 2017, p. 6).

In e-retailing, the principles of good governance must be synchronized with the principles for global e-retailing, taking into account the e-unique nature of e-retailing regarding security, privacy, redress, and jurisdiction. The principles of good governance for e-retailing are consistent with the eight basic consumer rights and with the OECD guidelines to protect e-consumers in terms of calling for self-regulation and initiatives by businesses and international coordination and collaboration.[3] In a democratic governance system, individual (e-consumers) and groups (CSOs) of citizens must be treated as both recipients and stakeholders in all governance and policy issues (Scholte 2002). Good governance allows the citizens' voice to be heard, whereas democracy enables citizens to participate in the policy-making process via the media, associations, consultation, and direct feedback (Holmes 2011). Good governance must reflect, serve, and protect fundamental democratic values which are very important to address the existing and new challenges associated with e-consumer protection.

Overall, these principles are relevant to e-consumer protection because they provide avenues for different groups of stakeholders to interact with each other to discharge governance more effectively. These principles cannot be accomplished by any single actor or different actors/sectors acting independently/autonomously. Thus, strong cooperation among all groups of stakeholders will carry forth good governance.

The Conventional Three-Sector Governance Framework for E-Consumer Protection

The following section discusses the three-sector governance framework to address e-consumer protection and its weaknesses. In the current governance framework for e-consumer protection, the key stakeholders currently are the state (government), the private sector (e-retailers), and CSOs.

---

[3] The eight basic consumer rights are the right to (i) safety, (ii) be informed, (iii) choose, (iv) be heard, (v) satisfaction of basic needs, (vi) redress, (vii) consumer education, and (viii) a healthy environment (NSW Office of Fair Trading undated).

Three Sectors in the Conventional Governance Framework

In the three-sector governance framework, not only does government have to demonstrate its obligation to citizens, but business also needs to demonstrate its CSR in order to enhance e-consumers' trust and confidence in online shopping (Figure 4.2). Besides, participation of CSOs is one of the requirements of a democratic society and for the development of good governance (OECD 2012).

Internationally, supranational organizations, such as the UN, the OECD, the EU, and APEC, have introduced a number of guidelines and directives in an attempt to deal with cross-border issues associated with e-retailing. At the national and subnational levels, the involved organizations have focused on special areas. For example, the ASEAN Committed on Consumer Protection and consumer protection agencies of various ASEAN member states are in charge of consumer affairs and fair trading issues. Many government agencies are also involved in this task, namely ministries of respected countries. However, these organizations focus at

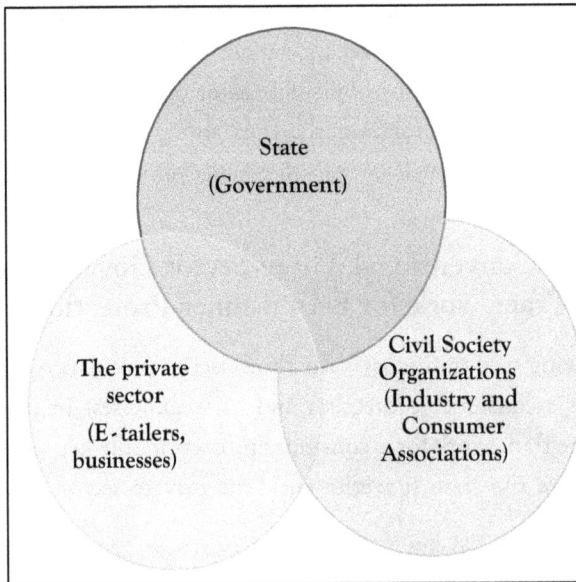

Figure 4.2 The conventional three-sector governance framework for e-consumer protection

Source: Adapted from Coghill (2004a), Ha (2011, 2012, 2017), and Shergold (2016)

the macro-level to protect national critical infrastructure. For example, the national and subnational offices of the Privacy Commissioners are responsible for privacy issues in both the offline and online markets. Finally, government agencies are usually involved in resolving disputes in the last stage when e-consumers and e-retailers are unable to settle their problems with or without assistance from an independent party. Each of the three sectors is discussed as follows.

The State

In this book, the state refers to government agencies which are involved in e-consumer protection. Government still has to play the main role in the proposed framework by focusing on setting the "rule of law." However, government needs to take into consideration the benefits of both e-consumers and e-retailers to achieve the principles of fair play and equity. Government also plays the central role of encouraging more participation and cooperation among all stakeholders and negotiating with other levels of government to address jurisdictional concerns and legislative harmonization. Government also needs to work with other groups to narrow the expectation gaps regarding self-regulation and provision of dispute resolution services (Ha 2012, 2017).

The Private Sector

The private sector refers to local and global e-retailers who operate in ASEAN countries and have e-customers in ASEAN or other countries. E-retailers are expected to comply with regulations, guidelines, and codes of practice and to exercise CRS by providing relevant information to customers and having proper internal policies and practices to handle customer's complaints (Ha 2012, 2017).

Civil Society Organizations

CSOs in this volume consist of international, national, and subnational industry and consumer associations. Internationally, CSOs, such as the ICPEN and Consumers International (CI), have actively worked with enforcement agencies of their member countries to conduct Internet check campaigns. These organizations have provided information about the current trends of online incidents to the public via their websites or via national government bodies. They have also provided online platforms for e-consumers to lodge their complaints. Most ASEAN countries have consumer associations. However, they usually focus on protection of consumers in general, not particularly e-consumers. Most of the industry associations also focus on their own areas of interests (Ha and McGregor 2013).

Although CSOs share similar functions, such as educating consumers and e-retailers and cooperating with other sectors to address e-consumer protection, each organization in this sector focuses on different areas. For example, industry associations establish industry codes of practice, whereas consumer associations advocate the rights of consumers. Given limited power to perform their duties, CSOs need support from government.

Weaknesses of the Conventional Governance Framework for E-Consumer Protection

The weaknesses of the conventional three-sector governance framework in successfully addressing e-consumer protection have centered around governance issues. These are mainly insufficient cooperation among different groups of stakeholders and lack of e-consumer participation.

First, the responsibilities of organizations regarding resolving cross-jurisdictional disputes have not been made clear. E-consumers are confused about which organizations they need to approach when they encounter problems with online shopping, especially cross-border transactions (World Economic Forum 2019). Inadequate information about the available channels of redress also contributes to undermining consumers' ability to seek remedies. The conventional governance framework cannot achieve good governance because of lack of accountability and the ineffectiveness of information disclosure regarding e-consumer protection by the relevant organizations.

Second, each organization has focused on individual issues among the issues associated with e-consumer protection. For instance, different agencies are in charge of e-security and privacy issues. These individual issues may be appropriately dealt with when they stand alone. However, they are not adequately addressed in e-retailing given their interdependence. For example, an insecure payment system could reveal consumers' information to a third party who may illegally use such information for committing an offence. Thus, an insecure payment system could lead to privacy breaches that may facilitate online identity theft. Consequently, addressing data and payment security could prevent privacy incidents from occurring. However, government has not adequately responded to these incidents as an integrated problem in e-retailing. Thus, a public–private partnership between government and the private sector is proposed to work with each other to enhance better level of e-security (Davis 2019).

Third, the lack of consensus among different government bodies has been reflected through different e-retailing-related standards, regulations, and guidelines in different jurisdictions (World Economic Forum 2019). This, in turn, makes the already weak enforcement of such standards, regulations, and guidelines more difficult. This means the "rule of law" exists, but regulations, guidelines, and standards are not effectively implemented. In other words, consumers receive different levels of protection from different e-retailers when they shop online and receive different levels of compensation when they seek redress.

Fourth, good governance is inhibited by insufficient participation of different groups of stakeholders and inadequate cooperation among the three sectors of governance. Lack of cooperation in e-retailing has been reflected via ineffective information dissemination and weak legal enforcement. Although there is some cooperation among government agencies, and between government agencies and CSOs, their activities have been project-based, that is, on an ad hoc basis.

Since all sectors are interdependent, lack of cooperation among them and lack of e-consumers' awareness lead to ineffective measures to address e-consumer protection (UNCTAD 2017). This makes it difficult for the relevant organizations to address the issues associated with e-consumer protection from both the macro and micro levels. It is also difficult for the relevant regulators to evaluate the effectiveness of the current policy framework given the lack of records of the complaints relating to e-transactions (Ha 2012, 2017).

There has been some cooperation among international CSOs (e.g., the ICPEN and the CI) and national government agencies. Although international CSOs have provided services and conducted activities to protect e-consumers, these activities have been limited. Educational campaigns are usually launched only after several similar incidents occurred. This indicates a reactive strategy rather than a proactive approach. Therefore, such organizations may be unable to identify new online risks and threats, report such incidents to the relevant government agencies, or provide timely information to consumers about new online threats.

In general, there has been a lack of international cooperation on laws and measures and a lack of cross-sector cooperation as suggested by the OECD (2019c). Also, consumers' participation in the governance framework was limited. Many consumers did not carry out necessary activities to protect themselves in the online environment. The three-sector governance framework only includes government, e-retailers, and CSOs, and the activities of each sector do not fully explain the operation of e-consumer protection. Consequently, this framework is not adequate for addressing the issues associated with e-consumer protection because of the weak links among sectors and the exclusion of e-consumers who have been directly affected by any consumer protection policies. The role of consumers in self-protection when shopping online and cooperation among all stakeholders to fulfill this challenging task should be taken into consideration. Thus, this study proposes the inclusion of e-consumers in the conventional three-sector governance framework.

A Proposed Four-Sector Governance Framework for E-Consumer Protection

This section proposes a "four-sector governance framework" including the original three sectors in society and adding e-consumers as an integrated segment for sustainable e-consumer protection. This section establishes a theoretical framework which is based on the main concept of the complex governance system in e-retailing and is supported by the subconcepts of (i) the roles of stakeholders, (ii) self-regulation in which corporate governance, CSR, and codes of practice are the main mechanisms, and

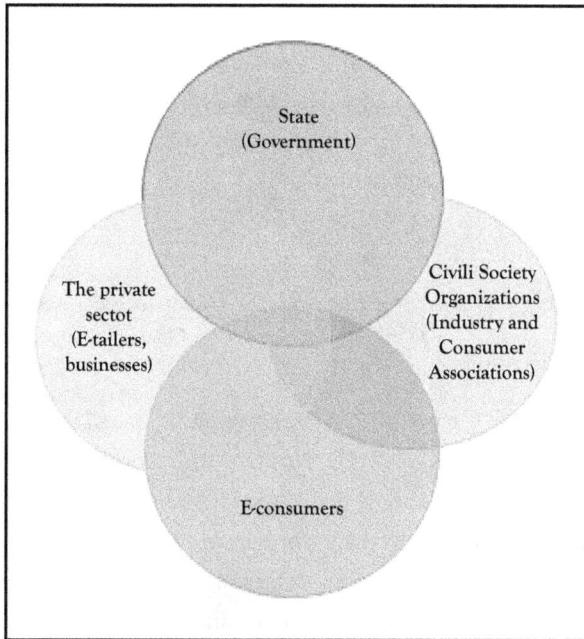

Figure 4.3 The proposed four-sector governance framework for e-consumer protection

(iii) participation by various groups of stakeholders, such as CSOs, consumer groups, and even e-consumers themselves. All these subconcepts aim to ensure that e-consumers can enjoy their basic rights, the same as consumers in traditional commerce, when they shop online. The proposed four-sector governance framework for e-consumer protection is presented in Figure 4.3.

In this proposed governance framework, government (the state) still has to play the main role in the protection of e-consumers. The private sector in the proposed framework is the same as in the current framework. E-retailers are expected to comply with regulations, guidelines, and codes of practice and to exercise CRS by providing relevant information to customers and having proper internal policies and practices to handle customers' complaints. CSOs in the proposed governance framework are the same as in the current three-sector governance framework.

However, e-consumers emerge as a distinct sector in the proposed four-sector governance framework. Nobody can help them make

decisions on whether to shop online or help them deal with online incidents when such incidents occur. If incidents occur, e-consumers have to
react instantly to protect themselves. They can only seek help to rectify
the problems afterwards. Thus, it is justified to include e-consumers in
the proposed governance framework.

Roles of Each Sector in the Four-Sector Governance Framework

Roles of Government

Fromkin (1999), Castro (2011), Crampton (2002), Farrell (2003),
Drezner (2004), Ha (2011, 2017), Ha and McGregor (2013), and World
Economic Forum (2019) argue that government has not been replaced by
the private sector in the governance of e-retailing. The main functions of
government include setting a legal framework, stimulating the economy,
assisting business, providing public goods and services, and cooperating
with other sectors.

First, government plays the main role in setting a legal framework,
comprising regulation and guidelines to enhance certainty and stability and keep business and society in order. Government establishes an
enabling environment for e-retailers to operate by setting the national
economic parameters such as contract law, national taxation system,
and fiscal and monetary policies (Ryan et al. 2003). Crampton (2002)
affirms that the basic needs of e-consumers "such as economic and
legal protection" have to be ensured by law and not by other forms
of regulation (pp. 12–13). Due to the cross-border nature of e-retailing, government needs to improve the current national structure to
match the global online trading systems. However, legislation cannot
work effectively without proper global compliance and enforcement
mechanisms (Bureau of Consumer Protection and Federal Trade Commission 2000). Intelligent but dishonest e-retailers can make use of
legislative loopholes (e.g., the exclusion of small businesses from the
Privacy Act) to conduct unfair trade practices and avoid legal obligations. Thus, government has to impose compliance through regulation, provided that government maintains legitimacy and "moral
authority" (Hall 1997).

Second, government has to facilitate the growth of markets by promoting the development of e-retailing via simple, predictable, but comprehensive and feasible guidelines (Froomkin 1999; United Nations ESCAP 2019). Government intervention is needed when there is market failure. Nevertheless, government can protect both e-consumers and e-retailers by providing mechanisms and incentives to encourage sufficient information disclosure, promoting competition, and calling for more socially responsible behavior by all stakeholders (World Commission on the Social Dimension of Globalization undated).

Third, government regulations can restrict behavior and prevent the occurrence or reoccurrence of certain undesirable activities, such as the unauthorized use of customers' personal data or credit card details for committing crimes (Froomkin 1999). However, government has to encourage research activities to develop new technological applications which can enhance the level of transaction security via the Internet and prevent intentional or unintentional harm to e-users (Productivity Commission (Australia) 2016).

Fourth, government assists businesses in negotiating with different levels of authorities to settle problems relating to e-consumer protection. Government has the capacity and authority to sign bilateral or multilateral agreements on jurisdiction and international redress (Cardoso 2004). Also, different jurisdictions create barriers to trade and "make it difficult for law-abiding suppliers to comply with various *consumer protection* laws" (Australian Competition and Consumer Commission 1999). Thus, there is a high demand for international standards, codes of conduct, and benchmarks to address e-consumer protection globally (Durovic 2020). Also, government has a role to play in the design, development, implementation, monitoring, and maintenance of new mechanisms of voluntary standards and codes since self-regulation could only work well if a strong compliance and monitoring regime exist (Castro 2011; OECD 2015).

Fifth, government can offer direct or indirect financial assistance to e-retailers and provide support services or infrastructure, for example, to develop security network systems or to enhance secure payment systems. In this field, there is a positive correlation between government involvement in the development of IT infrastructure and achievements of the collective objectives (World Economic Forum et al. 2005).

Finally, government agencies need to cooperate with other sectors and to promote cooperation between sectors and greater participation of stakeholders in the accomplishment of public policy objectives (Johnstone and Sarre 2004). In brief, government acts as a regulator and a policy maker, an economic stimulator, an assistant to business, a provider of goods/services, and a coordinator of the activities of different sectors.

Roles of E-Retailers

The process of globalization has transformed the economic setting in nearly every country (World Economic Forum et al. 2005). This transformation makes the private sector the nucleus of the economic and social development process. As of October 2019, there were 1.72 billion websites around the world (Armstrong 2019).

Given the current state of the global market, the main functions of e-retailers include creation of jobs and incomes, compliance with regulations and guidelines, and building trust. Considering the roles of e-retailers, first, firms have to operate in a legal and profitable manner. They need to consider the impacts on and contribution of their business activities to the welfare of other stakeholders. The manner in which they structure their organizations, the manner in which they operate business, and the way they communicate with and serve the stakeholders will affect their reputation and their performance and the outcomes of their corporate goals (World Economic Forum et al. 2005; World Economic Forum 2019).

Second, e-retailers can move beyond conformity with government regulation to create new values for e-consumers by demonstrating CSR and to effectively manage negative impacts, such as handling customers' complaints and meeting e-consumers' demand (Zarco-Jasso 2005; Anastasiadou, Lindh and Vasse 2019). New technologies can assist e-retailers to enhance engagement with e-consumers and also to enhance online payment security and privacy protection (Altamirano 2018).

Third, the globalization process has offered new opportunities to e-retailers, but also increased pressure on existing e-retailers by creating new competitors. In addition, recent e-security scandals have decreased public trust and corporate credibility (World Economic Forum et al.

2005; Unisys 2020). Thus, there is an increased demand for e-retailers to increase CSR efforts to maintain transparency and accountability in order to reinstate public trust and confidence. Not only do e-retailers have to achieve profit maximization to increase the share values, but they also need to protect the interests of the community and "consider society's larger goals" (McGregor 2019).

Overall, businesses act as job and wealth creators and trust and confidence builders within the realm of conformity to regulations and guidelines.

Roles of Civil Society Organizations

Although each group of CSOs, namely industry and consumer associations, may play different roles, they share some similar key functions. The first key function of CSOs is to limit the influence of governments (Office of Democracy & Governance (USAID) 2006). These organizations provide checks and balance on government's activities and power (UNDP-POGAR undated a). A way in which CSOs can enhance governance is by requesting more transparency, accountability, and efficiency from government. Indeed, CSOs have recently become so powerful and influential that "they literally have a place at the table along with government representatives" (Nalinakumari and MacLean 2005, p. 12).

By using "civil social pressure" or "civil regulations," CSOs can persuade or even force firms to adopt CSR practices (Harrison 2003, p. 130). Civil regulation refers to a situation where a CSO "sets the standard for business behavior" and firms can opt to take on or not to adopt these standards (Harrison 2003, p. 130). In some cases, the imposition of punitive measures by government may not affect the performance of companies, but actions from CSOs may generate serious financial loss to the public and the private sectors (World Economic Forum et al. 2005).

CSOs also scrutinize the activities of business in terms of the provision of goods and services. They monitor the level of honesty of e-retailers in advertising and assist enforcement agencies in investigating specific consumer complaints. If a firm is caught with "misleading advertising," its reputation may be seriously damaged (Borrie 2005, p. 65). CSOs also play an important role in the maintenance of public confidence "in the integrity of market transactions between business and a society" and the improvement of relationships between government and citizens (Ryan et al. 2003, p. 177).

Consumer groups also advocate the interests of consumers and to represent consumers through participation in public debates and the policy-making process (Teegen et al. 2004). These groups lobby for consumer rights on "competition, product information, product safety, citizen redress against unethical corporate behavior" (Ryan et al. 2003, p. 177). The OECD (2002b) affirmed that CSOs have contributed significantly to the protection of consumers. Many CSOs have been working with government and industry to address issues relating to online privacy protection, security, and unfair trading. For example, these organizations participated in the negotiation of the "Guidelines on Cryptography Policy (over 1996–1997) and the review of *the Guidelines on the Security of Information Systems and Networks* in 2001–2002" (OECD 2002, p. 8).

As many businesses are vulnerable to legal risks, they have acted to "protect their exposure to any potential shortcomings in their disclosure statements and practices" (Stefanic 2000, p. 4). To achieve this, they try to dilute the ability and attention of consumers to understand their practices by providing limited information. This also aims to defeat "the regulatory intent" (Stefanic 2000, p. 4). In such circumstances, to deserve the trust which consumers place on them, CSOs act as mediators between business and consumers. They take companies' data and present them in a practical and easy way which can help consumers make the best decisions (Peters 2005). To fulfill this role, CSOs have adopted the following main tools to "exert pressure on companies:

(a) consumer awareness campaigns—including boycotts of firms;
(b) investor awareness campaigns—including shareholder actions;
(c) direct action—including pickets, blockades and occupations;
(d) partnership approach—such as the World Wildlife Fund (WWF)" (Harrison 2003, p. 127).

These measures are sometimes more effective than government regulations since many CSOs can continuously pressurize firms and their campaigns can take place for an uncertain period of time (Asmus, Cauley, and

Maroney 2006). The coverage of these activities may be subnationwide, nationwide or worldwide.

The next function of CSOs is to educate e-consumers and e-retailers by disseminating information relating to "legal rights and redress, comparisons of products and services, or the actions of government and firms with respect to the delivery of products and services" to the public (Ryan et al. 2003, p. 1176). These groups alert consumers to unethical or unscrupulous traders and investigate suspected unfair trade practices.

Overall, CSOs can assist government, e-consumers, and e-retailers by playing match-making role between business (e-retailers) and society (e-consumers), between government and society, and between government and business. While CSOs have the propensity to maintain public confidence in government and in business, they can also help to increase public acceptance of public policy. They are an instrument for individuals to gain bargaining power in negotiating with business. They can also reduce the risks of financial loss and legal costs for e-retailers. In other words, they play an important role in governance and work with other groups of stakeholders to cocreate social values for the community.

Role of E-Consumers

E-consumers are able to protect themselves better by being aware of the risks associated with online shopping, having better knowledge of their rights and the available channels of redress, and exercising care before concluding an online transaction. However, most respondents in Group 1 (Consumers) failed to adequately protect themselves against online incidents. Thus, effective self-protection requires a very high level of consumers' ability and willingness to take precautions when shopping online. This also requires greater and better consumer education.

In addition, it is in the best interest of e-consumer to share both their negative and positive experiences with others via online forum or words of mouth to exert pressure on e-retailers for more transparency and accountability in the handling of consumers' complaints. This cooperation and social responsibility can be demonstrated by consumers by reporting online incidents to relevant organizations. Overall, e-consumers need to exercise consumer social responsibility.

Interdependence Among Sectors

A frictionless online marketplace with a high level of awareness of all stake-holders of common interest and "strong transactional integrity" would benefit both e-consumers and e-retailers (OECD 2002; Rotenberg 2001). E-retailing has been an emerging industry which can only be developed satisfactorily when consumers are confident in e-retailing and they are willing to purchase online. As e-transactions may be cross-border, international and national regulations cannot work well unless there are uniform regulation and proper mechanisms of law enforcement.

If law enforcement mechanisms are weak, some e-retailers will take advantage of many legal loopholes to gain unfair advantage in doing business. Therefore, self-regulation by the industry can help e-retailers voluntarily comply with their codes of practices. Yet, not all e-retailers can be induced by the industry to self-regulate, thus CSOs need to monitor the process and address the on-going problems (Harland 1999).

This kind of cooperation among parties must be prioritized because a proper regulatory framework would not only protect e-consumers but also be an engine for economic growth since such a legal framework can attract more investment. Cooperation is important in governing e-retailing because there are legal loopholes in many countries. All parties involving in e-transactions need the assurance and predictability that their transactions will be recognized and protected by laws (Sani 2002). Harmonization of laws regarding consumer protection would also contribute to achieving this objective of e-consumer protection (World Economic Forum 2019). According to the fourth consumer right, the voice of e-consumers must be heard directly, or through their representatives, and hence opinions of e-consumers must receive adequate attention, and e-consumers must be allowed to participate in the policy-making and implementation process.

Furthermore, all stakeholders should actively participate in shaping the impact and depth of the regulatory transformation to enhance e-consumer protection (Primo Braga 2004). However, national approaches may be insufficient to address e-consumer protection given the multifaceted nature of e-retailing. Hence, international resolutions must be explored (Centre for Credit and Consumer Law (Griffith University) 2004). Also, private initiatives and public–private partnerships play a main role in the development of technological applications, practices, and services in e-retailing (UNCTAD 2019).

Finally, the complex governance system must be able to operate at a global level. It is necessary to have an inclusive and comprehensive governance mechanism established on the "multi-stakeholder and multilateral basis" in order to internationalize e-retailing governance and settle unresolved matters in cross-border trade (Internet Society 2016).

The "four-sector governance framework" proposes that the separation of responsibilities and activities of each sector may not effectively enhance consumer confidence in e-retailing. Each of these sectors performs its own tasks, but they have to share a common duty to make the governance system function properly. These sectors work with one another to achieve good governance in protecting e-consumers.

Justification for the Proposed Four-Sector Governance Framework for E-Consumer Protection

Given the current state of e-consumer protection, the conventional three-sector governance framework does not produce the desirable outcomes, that is, insufficient protection of e-consumers, nor does it achieve the principles of good governance. In addition, the conventional governance framework does not specifically identify the position and the respective roles of e-consumers in the operations of the governance system.

In the conventional framework, consumers do not come into the picture as they have been represented by consumer associations. Since e-consumers are the main beneficiaries of the current policy framework for e-consumer protection, they do have a role to play. Although consumers are classified into the third sector (Holloway 1993), this study argues that e-consumers should be treated as a distinct sector in the governance framework to address e-consumer protection according to the principle of participation. They need to be self-reliant when shopping online. Although e-consumers can rely on consumer associations to voice their concerns and assist them in seeking redress, they have to make their own purchase decisions. They cannot ask their representatives to conclude a transaction for them. Since e-consumers are key actors in e-retailing, it is highly undesirable to omit them from any activities and programs which affect their well-being.

Arli and Tjiptono (2018), Ha (2011, 2017), and Levin (2013) posit that consumers have to demonstrate their social responsibility for addressing the issues associated with e-transactions by cooperating, sharing information and experience, and seeking redress. In a democratic society, every consumer has the right to participate in political, economic, and social activities. However, e-consumers cannot be empowered if they do not have any opportunities to directly participate in the policy-making and implementation processes regarding e-consumer protection and to know and exercise their basic consumer rights. In other words, empowering e-consumers means providing an opportunity for them to participate and to be responsible for their decisions to shop online. In traditional commerce, consumers usually know the name and address of a store, check with their relatives or friends about the credibility of the store/brand, and have to compare prices of the same products from different shops before they purchase an item. Thus, e-consumers can perform similar tasks in e-retailing with extra care. However, they have limited awareness and ability to provide self-help, thus other groups have to assist them. Overall, consumers must "take a much greater responsibility to take action to protect themselves" (Office of Communications (UK) 2006, p. 6).

Accordingly, to assist the analysis, the four-sector governance framework is proposed. This is an explanatory framework which emphasizes the important role of e-consumers in self-protection in e-retailing. The key players in the proposed framework are the same as those in the current framework, and e-consumers are added in as the fourth sector. This framework does not have the intention to alter the conventional governance framework in terms of institutions and structures, but the inclusion of e-consumers is treated as a mechanism to deliver policy outputs. This framework also emphasizes a stronger link among all sectors to fulfill their own duties and, at the same time, to achieve common goals. Also, effective e-consumer protection requires a higher level of international, national, and subnational cooperation and a "much higher degree of co- and self-regulation than" consumer protection in other forms of commerce (Office of Communications (UK) 2006). Improved e-consumer protection through stronger cooperation among sectors would be facilitated by the application of the proposed four-sector governance framework.

Strengths of the Proposed Four-Sector Governance Framework for E-Consumer Protection

The strengths of the proposed four-sector governance framework for e-consumer protection are subsequently discussed. First, well-defined responsibilities of organizations in various sectors involved in e-consumer protection could partially address nonuniform standards and regulations (Ha 2012, 2017). In response to this proposed framework, the respective organizations will be more accountable for their actions regarding e-consumer protection. Clearly defined responsibilities of relevant organizations will also enable e-consumers to be more confident in approaching them.

Second, individual issues of e-consumer protection have been addressed by different organizations; thus a central body to coordinate the activities of these organizations could help government focus and reallocate scare resources to protect e-consumers more efficiently. Strong cooperation among all involved parties could be an alternative if it is difficult to establish such a central agency.

Third, different standards and regulations were major concerns of the interviewees. This matter could be solved at the national and subnational levels though it requires strong political will from leaders and a special effort from the parties involved. However, this task is more complicated and challenging to be achieved at the international level. This issue could, however, be addressed by strong coordination and cooperation among different levels of government and different organizations.

Fourth, government needs to respond to consumer demand for effective e-consumer protection. Too many regulations will impede the development of e-retailing and incur compliance and enforcement costs to e-retailers and government, respectively. However, insufficient regulations disable enforcers from taking action against offending e-retailers and preventing offences from occurring. It is not only the number of regulations which matter (i.e., a large amount of regulation would increase red-tape and the cost of compliance), but also how regulations are enforced (Teubner 1983). Regulations could be complemented by e-retailers' effective adopting of self-regulatory mechanisms, such as guidelines and industry codes of practice. Cooperation among all sectors could then contribute to the successful implementation of regulations, guidelines, and industry codes regarding e-consumer protection.

Fifth, the lack of awareness of both e-consumers and e-retailers concerning the current policy framework for e-consumer protection, including self-protection and self-regulation, could be addressed by more education. Several channels of education are proposed, such as education by government via the mass media and by CSOs. E-retailers could also provide education to e-consumers via information posted on their websites (Office of Communications (UK) 2006). Peer-to-peer informal education is another feasible strategy to enhance public awareness of issues associated with e-retailing. However, educational programs can only be effective if the receivers are willing to obtain information and apply it. This requires the willingness of e-consumers and e-retailers to obtain relevant information from others to protect themselves and to provide protection to e-consumers, respectively. Multichannels of communication are necessary to achieve the objectives of public education regarding e-consumer protection.

Finally, official and timely evaluation of the implementation of regulations, guidelines, and codes of practice regarding e-consumer protection may help relevant organizations promptly identify the problems in the process(es) and revise and improve their process(es) to detect and deal with problems before they spin out of control.

Overall, cooperation among and participation of all sectors are key success factors to achieve better e-consumer protection. Solutions to address online shopping-related issues depend on the joint forces of both private and public organizations. They also depend on the degree of self-help by consumers (Grabosky 2001; Grabosky, Smith and Demsey 2001; Leven 2013; Small 2019). In sum, strong cooperation among all sectors would contribute to enhancing e-consumer protection (OECD 2004).

Conclusion

This chapter has integrated and discussed the conventional three-sector governance framework. First, there is a domino effect when consumer rights are violated, that is, the violation of one consumer right may lead to disrespect for another. This implies that all issues associated with e-consumer protection must be addressed simultaneously by various groups of stakeholders. Nonetheless, the conventional governance framework could not provide sufficient and effective explanation of protection to e-consumers. This is a result of its inherent weaknesses and the multifaceted issues associated with e-consume protection which rooted from a mixture of causes related to human behaviors, legality, and technology.

Thus, this study proposed a four-sector governance framework which consists of government, e-retailers, CSOs, and e-consumers. According to the proposed framework, cooperation among stakeholders and more consumer participation are the key instruments to achieve a higher level of acceptability from the public, a possible decrease in the number of complaints related to online shopping, and higher consumer trust and confidence in e-retailers. It is argued that cooperation among all groups could contribute to addressing the domino effects and reducing the expectation gaps, and consequently enhancing e-consumer protection. However, how consumers can be persuaded to take an informed interest in self-protection and participation is an issue which needs to be further explored.

The next chapter will discuss three case studies of how e-retailers protect their e-consumers in the context of ASEAN countries.

References

Albareda, L. 2008. "Corporate responsibility, governance and accountability: From self-Regulation to Co-regulation." *Corporate Governance* 8, no. 10, pp. 430–439.

Altamirano, A. 2018. "How Retail Is Utilising Technology to Keep Up with E-Commerce." *Forbes*, August 9, 2018. https://forbes.com/sites/forbestechcouncil/2018/08/09/how-retail-is-utilizing-technology-to-keep-up-with-e-commerce/#861aaf4635bc

Anastasiadou, E., C. Lindh, and T. Vasse. 2019. "Are Consumers International? A Study of CSR, Cross-Border Shopping, Commitment and Purchase Intent among Online Consumers." *Journal of Global Marketing* 32, no. 4, pp. 239–254.

Arli, D.I., and F. Tjiptono. 2018. "Consumer Ethics, Religiosity, and Consumer Social Responsibility: Are they Related?" *Social Responsibility Journal* 14, no. 2, pp. 302–320. doi: 10.1108/SRJ-03-2016-0036

Armstrong, M. 2019. "How Many Websites Are There?" *Statista,* October 28, 2019. https://statista.com/chart/19058/how-many-websites-are-there/

Asian Development Bank. 2000. *Promoting Good Governance: ADB's Medium-Term Agenda and Action Plan.* Asian Development Bank. http://adb.org/scripts/rwisapi.dll/@adb.env

Asmus, P., H. Cauley, and K. Maroney. 2006. "Turning Conflict into Cooperation." *Stanford Social Innovation Review* 4, no. 3, pp. 52–61.

Australian Competition and Consumer Commission. 1999. *US Perspectives on Consumer Protection in the Global Electronic Marketplace - Comment.* Washington, D.C.: Federal Trade Commission (US).

Australian Government's Overseas Aid Program (AusAID). 2000. *Good Governance: Guiding Principles for Implementation.* Canberra: The Australian Government's Overseas Aid Program (AusAID).

Borrie, L. 2005. "CSR and Advertising Self-regulation." *Consumer Policy Review* 15, no. 2, pp. 64–70.

Braithwaite, J., and P. Drahos. 2000. *Global Business Regulation.* Cambridge: Cambridge University Press.

Breslin, S. and H.E.S. Nesadurai. 2018. "Who Governs and How? Non-State Actors and Transnational Governance in Southeast Asia." *Journal of Contemporary Asia* 48, no. 2, pp. 187–203. doi: 10.1080/00472336.2017.1416423

Bruce-Lockhart, A. 2016. *What do we mean by 'governance'?* Geneva: World Economic Forum. https://weforum.org/agenda/2016/02/what-is-governance-and-why-does-it-matter/

Bureau of Consumer Protection and Federal Trade Commission. 2000. *Consumer Protection in the Global Electronic Market.* Federal Trade Commission (USA). https://ftc.gov/sites/default/files/documents/reports/consumer-protection-global-electronic-marketplace-looking-ahead/electronicm kpl.pdf

Butcher, J., and D. Gilchrist, eds. 2016. *The Three Sector Solution: Delivering Public Policy in Collaboration with Not-For-Profits and Business.* Australia: ANU Press. http://jstor.org/sta ble/j.ctt1rqc9kc

Cardoso, F.H. 2004. "Civil Society and Global Governance." *High Level Panel on UN-Civil Society, 26 July 2004.* Paris: UN Non-Governmental Liason Service.

Castro, D. 2011. *Benefits and Limitations of Industry Self-Regulation for Online Behavioral Advertising.* The Information Technology and Innovation Foundation. https://itif.org/files/2011-self-regulation-online-behavioral-advertising.pdf

Centre for Credit and Consumer Law (Griffith University). 2004. *Online Shopping and Consumer Protection.* Brisbane: Centre for Credit and Consumer Law, Griffith University.

Coghill, K. 2004a. "Federalism: Fuzzy Global Trends." *Australian Journal of Politics and History* 50, no. 1, pp. 41–56.

Coghill, K. 2004b. Governance Within a GlobaliSing Framework. In *The Australian Institute of International Affairs Victorian Branch, Global Challenges for the New Millennium Series,* Melbourne, VIC: Monash University, Monash Governance Research Unit.

Commission of the European Communities. 2001. *European Governance - A White Paper.* Brussels: Commission of the European Communities.

Crampton, S. 2002. "Consumer Protection in a Brave New World." *Consumer Policy Review* 12, no. 1, pp. 9–17.

Davis, J. 2019. "Massive SingHealth Data Breach Caused by Lack of Basic Security." *Health IT Security,* January 10, 2019. https://healthitsecurity.com/news/massive-singhealth-data-breach-caused-by-lack-of-basic-security

Drezner, D.W. 2004. "The Global Governance of the Internet: Bringing the State Back." *Political Science Quarterly* 119, no. 3, pp. 477–498.

Duch-Brown, N. 2017. *The Competitive Landscape of Online Platforms.* JRC Digital Economy Working Paper 2017-04. Seville, Spain: European Commission.

Durovic, M. 2020. "International Consumer Law: What Is It All About?" *Journal of Consumer Policy* 43, pp. 125–143. https://doi.org/10.1007/s10603-019-09438-9

Farrell, H. 2003. "Constructing the International Foundations of E-Commerce - The EU-U.S. Safe Harbour Arrangement." *International Organization* 57, no. Spring 2003, pp. 277–306.

Fox, J. 2007. "Government Transparency and Policymaking." *Public Choice* 131, no. 12, pp. 23–44.

Froomkin, A.M. 1999. "Of Governments and Governance." *Berkeley Technology Law Journal* 14, no. 2, pp. 1–9.

Governance Institute of Australia. 2020. *What is Governance?* Sydney: Governance Institute of Australia. https://governanceinstitute.com.au/resources/what-is-governance/

Grabosky, P. 2001. "Electronic Misappropriation and Dissemination of Personal Information." In *Electronic Theft: Unlawful Acquisition in Cyberspace.* Cambridge: Cambridge University Press 2001.

Grabosky, P., R.G. Smith, and G. Dempsey. 2001. *Electronic Theft: Unlawful Acquisition in Cyberspace.* Cambridge, New York: NY: Cambridge University Press.

Gupta, R. 2005. *A Public-Private Partnership to Build a Better World.* Paper read at The U.N. General Assembly, 14 Sep 2005, at New York, US.

Ha, H. 2011. "Security and Privacy in E-consumer Protection in Victoria, Australia." 5th International Conference on Trust Management (TM), 240–252. June 2011, Copenhagen, Denmark.

Ha, H. 2012. "Online security and consumer protection in Ecommerce - An Australian case." In *Strategic and Pragmatic E-Business: Implications for Future Business Practices,* ed. K. M. Rezaul, 217–243. Hershey, PA: IGI Global.

Ha, H. 2017. "Stakeholders' Views on Self-Regulation to Protect Consumers in E-Retailing." *Journal of Electronic Commerce in Organizations* 15, no. 3, pp. 83–103.

Ha, H., and S.L.T. McGregor. 2013. "Role of Consumer Associations in the Governance of E-commerce Consumer Protection." *Journal of Internet Commerce* 12, no. 1, pp. 1–25.

Hall, R.B. 1997. "Moral Authority as a Power Resource." *International Organization* 51, no. 4, pp. 591–622.

Harland, D. 1999. "The Consumer in the Globalized Information Society - The Impact of the International Organizations." *Australian Competition and Consumer Law Journal* 7, no. 23.

Harrison, R. 2003. "Corporate Social Responsibility and the Consumer Movement." *Consumer Policy Review* 13, no. 4, pp. 127–131.

Holmes, B. 2011. *Citizens' Engagement in Policymaking and the Design of Public Services*. Research Paper No. 1, 2011–12 (Parliament Library). Canberra: Commonwealth of Australia.

Huetter, P. 2004. *The State as First Among Equals: State-civil Society Relations in the Development Context*. Canberra: Centre for Democratic Institutions, Research School of Social Sciences, Australian National University. http://cdi.anu.edu.au/research_publications/research_down loads/Pierre Huetter_DevNetConference_Dec02.pdf.

IMF. 2020. *IMF and Good Governance*. Washington, D.C.: The IMF. https://imf.org/en/About/Factsheets/The-IMF-and-Good-Governance

Internet Society. 2016. *Internet Governance – Why the Multistakeholder Approach Works*. Reston, VA: Internet Society.

Jarrar, Y. 2017. *What is the Role of Government in the Digital Age?* Geneva: World Economic Forum.

Johnstone, R., and R. Sarre. 2004. *Regulation: Enforcement and Compliance*. Canberra: Australian Institute of Criminology.

Kaufmann, D., A. Kraay. and M. Mastruzzi. 2008. *Governance Matters VII: Aggregate and Individual Governance Indicators 1996–2007*. Washing D.C.: The World Bank.

Kooiman, J. 1999. "Socio-political Governance." *Public Management* 1, no. 1, pp. 67–92.

Kourula, A., J. Moon, M. Salles-Djelic. and C. Wickert. 2019. "New Roles of Government in the Governance of Business Conduct: Implications for Management and Organizational Research." *Organization Studies* 40, no. 8, pp. 1101–1123.

Lam, N.V. 2002/03. "A Perspective on Good Governance." In *Bulletin on Asia-Pacific Perspectives 2002/03. Asia-Pacific Economies: Sustaining Growth Amidst Uncertainties*. New York: UN, Economic and Social Commission for Asia and the Pacific.

Lee, J. 2019. *How Multistakeholder Platforms can Strengthen Our Multilateral System*. Geneva: World Economic Forum.

Levin, A. 2013. "The Best Form of Consumer Protection? Self-Protection." *Forbes*, April 29, 2013. https://forbes.com/sites/adamlevin/2013/04/29/the-best-form-of-consumer-protection-self-prote ction/#7493f5ff5bae

Lianos, I., D. Mantzari, G.M. Durán, A. Darr, and A. Raslan. 2019. *The Global Governance of Online Consumer Protection and E-commerce Building Trust*. Cologny/Geneva: *World Economic Forum*.

Mathiason, J., M. Mueller, H. Klein, M. Holitscher, and L. McKnight. 2004. *Internet Governance: The State of Play*. The Convergence Centre, Syracuse University School of Information Studies, the Moynihan Institute of Global Affairs of the Maxwell School of Syracuse University and the Internet and Public Policy Project (IP3), Georgia Institute of Technology.

McGregor, J. 2019. "Group of top CEOs says Maximizing Shareholder Profits No Longer can be the Primary Goal of Corporations." *The Washington Post*, August 30, 2020.

Midttun, A. 2004. "Corporate (Social) Responsibility: Governance in the Interface between Business, the State and Civil Society." Paper read at The European Academy of Business in Society - 3rd Annual Colloquium." The Challenge of Sustainable Growth: Integrating Societal Expectations in Business, September 2728, 2004, at Vlerick Leuven Gent Management School, Belgium.

Nalinakumari, B., and R. MacLean. 2005. "NGOs: A Primer on the Evolution of the Organizations that are Setting the Next Generation of 'Regulations'." *Environmental Quality Management* 14, no. 4, pp. 1–21.

Nooren, P., N. van Gorp, N. van Eijik, and R.O. Fathaigh. 2018. "Should We Regulate Digital Platforms? A New Framework for Evaluating Policy Options." *P&I: Policy and Internet* 10, no. 3, pp. 264–301. doi: 10.1002/poi3.177

NSW Office of Fair Trading. undated. *International Consumer Rights: The World View on International Consumer Rights*. Parramatta: NSW Office of Fair Trading. https://fairtrading.nsw.gov.au/help-centre/youth-and-seniors/youth/international-consumer-rights

OECD. 2002. "Civil Society and the OECD." *The Observer, OECD*, 112. November 2002. OECD. 2004. *Summary of Responses to the Survey on the Implementation of the OECD Guidelines for the Security of Information Systems and Networks: Towards a Culture of Security (DSTI/ICCP/REG(2003)8/FINAL)*. Paris: OECD.

OECD. 2009. *Consumer Education: Policy Recommendations of the OECD'S Committee on Consumer Policy*. Paris: OECD.

OECD. 2012. *Partnering with Civil Society 12 Lessons from DAC Peer Reviews*. Paris: OECD.

OECD. 2013. *Trust in Government, Policy Effectiveness and the Governance Agenda.* In *Government at a Glance 2013.* Paris: OECD.

OECD. 2015. *Industry Self-Regulation: Role and Use in Supporting Consumer Interests.* Paris: OECD.

OECD. 2018a. *Implications of E-commerce for Competition Policy - Note by BIAC.* Paris: OED.

OECD. 2018b. *OECD Draft Policy Framework on Sound Public Governance.* Paris: OECD.

OECD. 2019c. *Challenges to Consumer Policy in the Digital Age.* Paris: OECD.

Peters, M. 2005. "CSR is a Consumer Concern." *Consumer Policy Review* 15, no. 2, pp. 36–37.

Primo Braga, C.A. 2004. "E-Commerce Regulation: New Game, New Rules?" Paper read at The Regulation of Development and the Development of Regulation Conference, April 23–24, 2004, at University of Illinois.

Productivity Commission (Australia). 2016. *Digital Disruption: What do Governments Need to do?* Commission Research Paper. Canberra: Productivity Commission (Australia).

Pyone, T., H. Smith and N. van den Broek. 2017. "Frameworks to Assess Health Systems Governance: A Systematic Review." *Health Policy and Planning* 325, 710–722. doi: 10.1093/hea pol/czx007

Rhodes, R.A.W. 1996. "The New Governance: Governing without Government." *Political Studies* 44, pp. 652–667.

Rotenberg, M. 2001. "Confidence and E-commerce." *The OECD Observer (OECD)* January 2001, no. 224, pp. 53–54.

Ryan, N., R. Parker, and K. Brown. 2003. *Government, Business and Society.* NSW: Person Education Australia.

Sacks, R.J. 1996." Rebuilding Civil Society: A Biblical Perspective." *The Responsive Community* 7, no. 1, p. 16.

Sadowsky, G., R. Zambrano, and P. Dandjinou. 2004. *Internet Governance: A Discussion Document prepared for the United Nations ICT Task Force.* New York: The United Nations ICT Task Force.

Sahut, J., M. Peris-Ortiz, F. Teulon, and S. Boubaker. 2019. "Corporate Social Responsibility and Governance." *Journal of Management and Governance* 23, no. 4, 901912. doi: 1007/s10997-019-09472-2.

Salmenkaita, J.P., and A. Salo. 2002. "Rationales for Government Intervention in the Commercialization of New Technologies." *Technology Analysis & Strategic Management* 14, no. 2, pp. 183–200.

Sani, R. 2002. "Changing Laws for E-commerce Push." *Computimes Malaysia,* p. 1.

Scholte, J.A. 2002. "Civil Society and Democracy in Global Governance." *Global Governance* 8, pp. 281–304.

Shergold, P. 2016. "Three Sectors, One Public Purpose." In *The Three Sector Solution: Delivering Public Policy in Collaboration with Not-For-Profits and Business* eds. J.R. Butcher. and D.J. Gilchrist, 2332. Canberra: ANU Press.

Shleifer, A. 2005. "Understanding Regulation." *European Financial Management* 11, no. 4, pp. 439–451.

Small, B. 2019. *Self-Defense Against Scams.* Federal Trade Commission, September 30, 2019. https://consumer.ftc.gov/blog/2019/09/self-defense-against-scams-0

Sriskandarajah, D. 2017. *Big business and activists finally agree. On this one issue at least.* Geneva: World Economic Forum. https://weforum.org/agenda/2017/06/activism-civil-society-good-for-business/

Stefanic, M. R. 2000. *The Role of Government in E-commerce.* US Federal Trade Commission, 22 February 2000. http://ftc.gov/acoas/comments/stefanic.htm.

Stocker, G. 1998. *Governance as Theory: Five Propositions.* UNESCO.

Teegen, H., J. P. Doh, and S. Vachani. 2004. "The Importance of Nongovernmental Organizations (NGOs) in Global Governance and Value Creation: An International Business research Agenda." *Journal of International Business Studies* 35, pp. 463–483.

The Nielsen Company (US), LLC. 2018. *Future Opportunities in FMCQ E-Commerce: Market Drivers and Five-Year Forecast.* New York: The Nielsen Company (US), LLC.

UN Secretary-General's High-level Panel on Digital Cooperation. 2019. *The Age of Digital Interdependence.* New York: UN.

UNDP. 1997. *UNDP and Governance: Experiences and Lessons Learned.* Management Development and Governance Division, United Nations Development Program.

UNDP-POGAR. 2006. *Democratic Governance, Participation: Civil Society.* UNDP-POGAR. http://pogar.org/governance/civil.asp.

United Nations Economic and Social Commission for Asia and the Pacific. 2005. *What is Good Governance?* United Nations Economic and Social Commission for Asia and the Pacific (UNESCAPE).

Unisys. 2020. 2020 *Unisys Security Index: Consumers' Security Concerns Globally.* Unisys. https://assets.unisys.com/Documents/Microsites/USI2020/Unisys SecurityIndexReport2020.pdf?v=2

UNCTAD. 2017. *Consumer Protection in Electronic Commerce.* New York: UNCTAD.

UNCTAD. 2019. *Digital Economy Report 2019: Value Creation and Capture: Implications for Developing Countries.* New York: UNCTAD.

United Nations ESCAP. 2019. *Selected Issues in Cross-Border E-Commerce Development in Asia and the Pacific.* Bangkok: United Nations ESCAP.

Weiss, T. M. 2000. "Governance, Good Governance and Global Governance: Conceptual and Actual Challenges." *Third World Quarterly* 21, no. 5, pp. 795–814.

Wilson, E.J. 2005. "What is Internet Governance and Where Does it Come From?" *Journal of Public Policy* 25, no. 1, pp. 29–50.

World Commission on the Social Dimension of Globalization. undated. *A Fair Globalization: Creating Opportunities for All*. World Commission on the Social Dimension of Globalization.

World Conference on Governance. 1999. "1999 Manila Declaration on Governance." *Commonwealth Innovations* 5, no. 3, pp. 8–9.

World Economic Forum, International Business Leaders Forum, and John. F. Kennedy School of Government, H.U. 2005. *Partnering for Success. Business Perspectives on Multistakeholder Partnership*. Cologny/Geneva: World Economic Forum.

World Economic Forum. 2017. *Agile Governance Reimagining Policy-making in the Fourth Industrial Revolution*. Geneva: World Economic Forum.

World Trade Organization. 2020. *E-Commerce, Trade and the Covid-19 Pandemic*. Geneva: World Trade Organization.

Zarco-Jasso, H. 2005. *Public-Private Partnerships: A Multidimensional Framework for Contracting*. Barcelona: IESE Business School, Universidad de Navarra.

CHAPTER 5

Case Studies of E-Consumer Protection in ASEAN

Introduction

The previous chapters have discussed the current governance framework and proposed an extension governance framework that includes e-consumers. This chapter aims to strengthen the justification for the proposed framework by examining how the selected e-retailers comply with the existing regulations and practice e-consumer protection, and the importance of cooperation among all sectors in the proposed governance framework to improve e-consumer protection in e-retailing. To accomplish this, the chapter explores three case studies of how popular e-retailers in ASEAN countries protect e-consumers. According to Austrade (2019), Statista (2020), and ASEAN UP (2019), Lazada group, Shopee, and Zalora are the top three most-visited e-retailers' websites across six ASEAN countries in 2019 and 2020. Thus, there is strong justification for the inclusion of these e-retailers in this chapter.

The case study method was selected for the following reasons. First, case studies are suitable techniques to address policy-related problems (Velder, Jansen and Anderson 2004). Second, case studies help researchers understand more about certain facts and incidents and develop "the type of context-dependent knowledge" (Flyvbjerg 2006). Such facts can help researchers "originate the findings for further empirical testing" (Bryman and Bell 2003, p. 56). Furthermore, as explained by Hancook and Algozzine (2006), insights derived from case studies can directly or indirectly influence future research directions. The advantage of the case studies in this chapter is to allow the author to be in the position of e-consumers to understand e-consumers' expectation when shopping online and to compare the theoretical framework with industry practices. Secondary data were found from the websites and annual reports of the selected e-retailers, and third parties' reports. Information was also obtained from industry news and independent websites that provide consumers' rating and reviews.

This chapter includes three cases. The first case elaborates how e-consumers are protected by Lazada (Singapore) with regard to information disclosure, privacy and security, redress, and jurisdiction. The second case analyzes how Shopee (Vietnam) handles its customers' complaints and addresses the issues associated with noncompliance by sellers. The final case focuses on online privacy and security of Zalora (Malaysia).

Lazada Group (Singapore) (www.lazada.sg)

Lazada (Singapore) was established in 2012, and its major shareholder is Alibaba Group Holding Limited, a Chinese multinational technology corporation (MNTC). It adopts three main e-business models, namely B2C, direct sales, and C2C. Its offers nearly every product category, ranging from computer products, electronics, food and beverages, fashion, skin care and healthcare products, to household products. It operates in six ASEAN countries: Indonesia, Malaysia, the Philippines, Singapore, Thailand, and Vietnam (Austrade 2019). This case study focuses on customers' perspective of Lazada's website, including LazMall and RedMart, in Singapore due to its top position in the country (Statista 2020).

Information Disclosure

A direct search for information on Lazada's website and its subsites (e.g., LazMall and RedMart) reveals that customers can conveniently search for several types of information about products posted on its website. At the bottom of the main web page, there are two groups of information, namely "Customer Care" and "Lazada." Information about *presales, sales, and postsales transactions* can be found from various links under the first set of information, "Customer Care." Its customers can find guidelines about how to start a purchase under the link "How to Buy" and information about shipping and delivery, refunds, returns, payments, own account login, products, LazMall, data privacy, Lazada community policies, and many others under the link "Lazada Help Center" and "RedMart Help

Centre."[1] There are also separate links for customers to check about shipping and delivery[2] as well as returns.[3] E-customers can also find information about "International Product Policy"[4] on Lazada's website. In addition, information about delivery options, return, and warranty is also exhibited on the webpage when customers can select and purchase a product.[5]

Information about *products* can be clearly found on its website, together with photos, descriptions, and even reviews and ratings by buyers. E-customers who are not IT-savvy or are first-time users are often confused or worried about complex purchasing procedures or technical issues and can find important and useful information on Lazada's website. However, e-customers whose English proficiency is not high or are not used to reading long documents may be discouraged to read all the guidelines or instructions. Partners that provide payment methods and delivery services to Lazada and its customers are displayed clearly on its website.

Lazada and its subsite RedMart do provide online links for customers to make queries on their order status and cancelled and returned order items. Customers have to log in their accounts in order to contact Lazada online. Lazada also provides "live chat" to assist customers. Those who are not well versed with searching for information on its website can contact its hotline service during office hours.

Information about *business registration* of Lazada can be found under the second set of information, "Lazada." A physical contact address and a location map in Singapore are posted on Lazada's website (Lazada Group 2019a).

---

[1] See https://lazada.sg/helpcenter/?spm=a2o42.11638377.footer_top.1.287f2dd1XJ 126U (accessed on 5 Sep 2020)

[2] See https://lazada.sg/helpcenter/shipping_delivery/?spm=a2o42.11638377.footer_ top.4.287f2dd1Lirg2o (Accessed on 5 Sep 2020)

[3] See https://lazada.sg/helpcenter/returns/?spm=a2o42.11638377.footer_top.6. 287f2dd1kCepdN#answer-faq-retu rn-ans (Accessed on 5 Sep 2020)

[4] See https://lazada.sg/helpcenter/products_on_lazada/?spm=a2o42.11638377. footer_top.5.287f2dd1HypaXZ#ans wer-faq-internationalproduct-ans (Accessed on 5 Sep 2020)

[5] An example can be seen at https://www.lazada.sg/products/rb-tea-milk-tea-w-brown-sugar-pearls-i610048363-s1787598434.html?spm=a2o42.searchlist. list.2.51d87dbfhB3jz4&search=1 (Accessed on 5 Sep 2020)

As Lazada is an e-retailer providing an online platform for sellers and buyers to engage in online transactions, there are general *terms and conditions* for purchasing via the platform.[6] Information about formation of contracts, orders, price and payment, delivery, warranty, liability, force majeure, and other general terms is provided in the *Terms and Conditions of Sales*[7] under the general terms and conditions section and is also subject to terms and conditions by sellers.

Apart from the two-way channels of *communication,* that is, (i) customers to Lazada and (ii) Lazada to customers, Lazada also provides online forums for members and community to communicate with one another. Policies with regard to communication among members of Lazada community are stated clearly on its website.[8]

Privacy and Security

Lazada posts its privacy policy on its website, as required by the current privacy legislation in Singapore. Lazada's privacy policy is available via a separate link on its website.[9] Lazada provides information about what types of personal information will be collected. Similar to other e-retailers, it claims to collect, use, disclose, store, and/or process customers' information in accordance with its privacy policy (Lazada Group 2019b), such as to process orders, deliver products, and provide service and support (Ha 2012, 2013, 2017). Lazada claims that customers are allowed to withdraw their consent for it to continue using, disclosing, and/or processing their data.

Lazada advises that "the platform may contain links to other websites operated by other parties, such as our business affiliates, merchants or payment gateways. We are not responsible for the privacy practices of

---

[6] See https://www.lazada.sg/terms-of-use/?laz_trackid=2:mm_150110918_5160 2155_2010602160:clk5gjnfil eh f03at2cevh (accessed on September 5, 2020)

[7] See https://lazada.sg/terms-of-use/?spm=a2o42.helpcenter-article.article-content.1. 3ed17bb9ZGLeWv (accessed on September 6, 2020)

[8] See https://lazada.sg/helpcenter/lazada-community-policies/?spm=a2o42.helpcenter.topics-list.11.486 6455feOrC St (Accessed on September 5, 2020)

[9] See https://lazada.sg/privacy-policy/?spm=a2o42.11638377.footer_top.15.2803 2dd1TVUhIa (accessed on September 5, 2020)

websites operated by these other parties" (Lazada Group 2019b). There is no article/clause in this privacy policy stating that its employees must protect the confidential relationship between Lazada and its customers, suppliers, and other groups of stakeholders. A phone number is provided on its website so that customers can freely contact it for any privacy and security issues (Lazada Group 2019b).

Lazada claims that it has adopted "appropriate administrative, physical and technical measures" to ensure online security; for instance, (i) only authorized persons can access customers' personal data; (ii) "maintaining technology products to prevent unauthorized computer access; and using 128-bit SSL (secure sockets layer) encryption technology" when it processes customers' financial information (Lazada Group 2019b).

Concerning payment security, Lazada has posted a payment protection policy on its website.[10] Its customers can choose different modes of payment, such as credit card (Visa/Master/American Express), Lazada wallet, and installment payment plan. Lazada advises that all payments must be made on its platform, and any requests to make payment offsite by sellers should be reported to it (Lazada Group undated a). E-transactions via Lazada's website are secured by industry-standard SSL technology. As explained by Franck Vervial, head of Cybersecurity Operations at Lazada, Lazada has invested significantly to improve its cybersecurity in order to protect its customers' personal and financial data (Barker 2017; French Chamber Singapore 2019). Also, Lazada's Information Security Management System (ISMS) meets the requirements of ISO/IEC 27001:2013 as certified by BSI U, and Lazada's payment system has also complied with the PCI QSA (Lazada Group 2019c).

Redress and Jurisdiction

Lazada's online terms and conditions state that the use of its platform and/or services and the terms and conditions "shall be governed by and construed in accordance with Singapore law and you hereby submit to the exclusive jurisdiction of the Singapore courts" (Lazada Group undated b).

---

[10] See https://lazada.sg/terms-of-use/?spm=a2o42.helpcenter-article.article-content.1. 64407bb9f4u723 (accessed on September 6, 2020)

Lazada highly recommends that customers and relevant parties try to discuss any problems and "resolve the dispute through amicable negotiations" first, and such dispute resolution processes should be conducted on "an individual basis" (Lazada Group undated b). Lazada provides a channel for customers to lodge a dispute to it via an app or an online form.[11] This demonstrates that Lazada has taken customer feedback seriously and has tried to internally and satisfactorily handle customer complaints. Lazada also explains that any external disputes or claims shall be settled by "arbitration in accordance with the Rules for Arbitration of the Singapore International Arbitration Centre (SIAC)" (Lazada Group undated b).

Customer Experience

In an exclusive interview for the Singapore Economic Development Board (2016), Lazada's then CEO, Martell Hardenberg, explained that Lazada's e-consumers are well protected with its "Buyer Protection, Money Back Guarantee, 100% Satisfaction Guaranteed return policies and integrated customer service team"; and this "sets us [Lazada] apart in the e-commerce field and helps ensure that customers benefit from a safe and convenient online shopping experience" (Singapore Economic Development Board 2016).

Lazada employs a strong team of data scientists that adopt big data and the latest technology to help it "make decisions about how to enhance, streamline, and personalize the user experience from the browsing stage to the point of purchase. Such optimization will improve the journey, customer experience and obviously overall sales" (Teh 2017). As a trusted brand in Southeast Asia, many big brands, such as Under Armour (Singapore and Thailand), Starbucks, and 3M Co (Indonesia) have recently worked with LazMall to sell their products online (*The Straits Times* 2020). Using artificial intelligence technology to personalize customer experience and improve customer satisfaction is one of its strengths (*The Straits Times* 2020). Lazada explained that it has taken and addressed its customers'

---

[11] See https://lazada.sg/helpcenter/How-do-I-submit-a-dispute%E2%80%8B. html#:~:text=Once%20your%20request%20has%20been,for%20your%20dispute%20and%20submit. (accessed on September 6, 2020)

feedback seriously because it wanted to offer the best user experience to its customers (Retailnews.asia 2019). Lazada has removed listings of unauthorized or counterfeit products (e.g., removing listings of unauthorized Microsoft software) from its platform to ensure that customers will not encounter buying fake/unlicensed products (Baharudin 2020).

Positive e-consumer experience with Lazada has been evidenced by the increased volume of sales of Lazada and its ranking (The ASEAN Post 2018). Lazada has a big market share in the region, and the number of visitors to its website increased 13 percent in 2019 (Singapore Business Review 2019). In 2020, Lazada Singapore received a silver award for the category of "Best Engagement for a Targeted Community" and a bronze award for the category of "Best PR Campaign: Services" by Marketing Magazine (2019 to 2020).

Regarding negative experiences, many customers have gone public with complaints by posting negative feedback on Lazada. Customers complained about common issues faced by any e-retailers, such as late or no delivery, poor quality of customer service and product, pricing issues which include problems with refunds, and poor technical support. On September 6, 2020, in a forum from hardwarezone.com.sg, which is part of the SPH Magazines Pte Ltd., 165 posts about Lazada were found. The latest post was on September 3, 2020, complaining about late delivery and customers being told either to wait or cancel the order.[12]

Pissedconsumer.com,[13] a consumer advocacy and review platform owned by Consumer Opinion LLC (registered in Las Vegas, NV), provides some consumers' reviews and rating of Lazada Singapore. For example, the first consumer's review of Lazada in this site was on January 22, 2015, and there are 320 reviews as of September 6, 2020 (Pissed Consumer 2020). The overall rating of this company is about 2 (out of 5), and those who write a review on this website were generally not satisfied with its shipping and delivery, return/replace, and refund as explained by Pissed Consumer (2020).

---

[12] See https://forums.hardwarezone.com.sg/hardware-clinic-2/horrible-shopping-experience-lazada-5673038-11.html (accessed September 6, 2020)

[13] See https://lazada-singapore.pissedconsumer.com/review.html (accessed September 6, 2020)

Specifically, a customer claimed that his personal data was not kept confidential because Lazada's CEO personally called him "after failed purchase Facebook post went viral" (How 2019). However, these may be few exceptional cases that attracted the public's attention and reaction.

Shopee (Vietnam) (https://shopee.vn/)

Shopee was launched in 2015 by the Sea Group, and its headquarter is in Singapore. It adopts two main e-business models, namely B2C and C2C. Similar to Lazada, it offers a wide range of product categories, for example, computer products, electronics, food and beverages, fashion, skin care and healthcare products, and household products. It operates in Indonesia, Malaysia, the Philippines, Singapore, Thailand, Vietnam, and Taiwan (Austrade 2019). Shopee in Vietnam will be the focus of this case study as it was ranked number one in Vietnam (Do 2019). E-consumers can search Shopee's website in English or Vietnamese.

Information about *products, presales, sales, and postsales* transactions is available on Shopee's website. Its *business contact, terms and conditions,* and *privacy policy* are also posted online. However, *Shopee has been found to* exhibit many constraints with regard to protecting consumers from poor quality and fake goods (Hara 2020). In some occasions, prohibited products were found to be on Shopee's website although sellers are not allowed to do so by Shopee (VietNamNet 2019). Yet, it seems some sellers did take advantage of the *loose administration of Shopee.* The Vietnam Competition and Consumer Authority (VCCA) under the Ministry of Industry and Trade (MoIT) have handled about 568 complaints from e-consumers, and most of them were from big e-retailers. *Recently, several e-consumers have complained about fake products and overpriced products sold on Shopee's platform, and they also failed to get compensation or adequate protection from the company (Hara 2020).* There were cases that "a package of 100 Japanese medical face masks was offered for VND2.7 million ($120) on Shopee, about 10 times higher than the market price from before the pandemic" (Hara 2020). However, Shopee quickly removed such a post from its platform after receiving complaints from customers about the overpricing. It has closely worked with authorities in Vietnam to identify sellers who inflated the price of face masks and hand sanitizers during COVID-19. So far, Shopee has removed about "3,700 stores and about 4,800 masks and hand sanitisers" listed on its platform (Sachitanand 2020).

Shopee also blocked the accounts of vendors who violated its terms and conditions, for instance, selling fake or prohibited products. *Shopee (undated) has committed to resolving disputes by hiring staff for its* "Operations—Customer Service (Cross Border Dispute)."[14] This department is in charge of handling customers' queries and complaints, resolving issues arising during cross-border transactions. Importantly, the team should be "the voice" of customers to provide feedback to the sellers. Apparently, Shopee understands that protecting e-consumers can help it avoid regulatory costs and protect its business sustainability.

However, e-consumers have perceived that Shopee did not take action fast enough to protect its customers from "ghost" vendors (Van Anh 2019). As a result, a huge amount of money has been cheated from its customers. It took Shopee several days to block a "ghost" vendor's accounts after receiving complaints from hundreds of its customers (Van Anh 2020). This demonstrates Shopee's shortcomings in addressing redress.

Zalora (Malaysia) (www.zalora.com.my)

Zalora was launched in 2012 and is owned by the Global Fashion Group. It has headquarters in both Malaysia and Singapore (Tee 2019). It adopts three main e-business models, namely B2C, direct sales, and C2C. Different from Lazada and Shopee, its main and only product category is fashion. It operates in four ASEAN countries—Indonesia, Malaysia, the Philippines, and Singapore—and also in Hong Kong and Taiwan (Austrade 2019). Zalora in Malaysia is the nexus of the discussion in this case study as it offers products differently from Lazada and Shopee and was among the top five websites in Malaysia.

Zalora Malaysia has posted clear personal data protection policy in both English and Bahasa Malaysia. This policy explains how Zalora collects, uses, and shares its customers' personal data. This policy is more detailed than other e-retailers'. For example, Zalora provides "governing

---

[14] See https://careers.shopee.sg/job-detail/1736/ (accessed on September 7, 2020)

law" of its privacy policy, that is, in Malaysia, whereas Shopee Vietnam does not do so (Zalora 2019). It also provides a link to an e-mail and a physical office address for customers to contact it when there are issues of privacy. However, it seems that many people can access its customers' personal information as stated in the policy, even temporary workers, although it claims to do the best to "minimize the disclosure of [customers'] personal data to the information necessary to perform the related purpose or additional purpose" (Zalora 2019). Its customers can access and/or correct their personal data and withdraw their consent for Zalora to collect, use, and share their personal information.[15]

A number of articles have written about how Zalora dealt with an alleged leaking of its customers' personal data. In 2014, an individual seller claimed that he had wanted to sell 900,000 accounts of Zalora's customers (AsiaOne 2014). However, Zalora rebuked that it has always and seriously protected customers' data privacy, and its customer database "is extremely secure and has never been sold, monetized or shared with third parties" (AsiaOne 2014). There is a tab "Responsible Disclosure" on Zalora's website where customers can find an e-mail to report any security incidents to Zalora.[16] Zalora has encouraged its customers to cocreate a safe and secure online shopping environment by asking customers to report any potential security vulnerabilities to it.

In 2017, Zalora encountered another rumor pertaining to the WannaCry ransomware cyberattack in which the attackers locked the affected computers and held users' files for ransom. Zalora affirmed to its customers that it was not affected by this incident (Murugiah 2017). To respond to customers' concerns, Zalora introduced an alternative payment option, that is, "cash on delivery," so that customers do not need to reveal their financial information online (Murugiah 2017). Zalora also ensured that its security systems are frequently updated and enforced its internal security policies. It has also educated employees with regard to cybersecurity.

Zalora has been able to regain trust from customers and acquire new customers even during the COVID-19 lockdown (A Malek 2020). In April 2020, Zalora was ranked fifth among the leading e-commerce

---

[15]   See https://zalora.com.my/privacy-policy/#law (accessed on September 8, 2020)

[16]   See https://zalora.com.my/responsible-disclosure/(accessed September 8, 2020)

platforms during the lockdown in Malaysia (Statista 2020). This is a big achievement of Zalora given that it only sells fashion products.

Discussion

The case studies demonstrate that the three e-retailers do comply with the legal requirements in the respective countries. However, there were incidents that displayed the weaknesses in their systems and processes. Analyses of these e-retailers reveal the following key findings.

First, these e-retailers have complied with the legal requirements in the respective countries in terms of providing information about products, business, payment methods, transaction processes, presales and postsales services, including refunds/exchanges, shipping, and delivery. Although the volume of the relevant information varies among e-retailers, most of the necessary information is available to e-customers for them to make informed decisions. Nonetheless, e-retailers have limited capacity to identify, monitor, and block the accounts of fraudulent sellers who want to do unethical business by selling fake products or overpriced products, especially during the COVID-19 lockdown. Thus, the principle of *caveat emptor* still prevails in the online market. This strengthens the justification to include e-consumers in the proposed multisector governance framework.

Second, these e-retailers have posted privacy policies and information about how customers' personal and financial data are protected. They have also explained how technologies are adopted to improve online security. Importantly, they have provided a link, a phone number, or an e-mail for their customers to contact them for any online security breach or potential security breach. Yet, e-retailers should identify potential security breaches and take proactive measures to prevent such incidents instead of being reactive to respond to them only after such incidents occur.

Third, redress mechanisms and internal policies for customers to seek redress are available. However, the implementation of such policies varies vastly. In some cases, it took longer time for e-retailers to address the issues. In other cases, e-retailers had to work with the authorities to address such issues. However, very few alternative dispute resolution options have been stated by these e-retailers. This offers opportunities for further research on redress in e-retailing.

Conclusion

This chapter discusses three case studies of the top e-retailers in the respective ASEAN countries, namely, Lazada Singapore, Shopee Vietnam, and Zalora Malaysia. Apparently, these cases demonstrate that well-known e-retailers do attempt to build trust and protect their e-customers in order to retain existing e-customers and attract new e-customers. Yet, they do have their limitations. In many cases, e-retailers need to call for contribution by e-consumers, and cooperation by various groups of stakeholders, including the authorities and the industry. Thus, further improvement by e-retailers, pertaining to internal policies and processes, and technological adoption are required for a safe and secure online marketplace. Although e-consumers can seek help from respective stakeholders, they ultimately must make decisions by themselves when they make purchases online. Therefore, they need to take caution when they are online.

This chapter only includes three cases of well-known e-retailers in ASEAN countries. Yet, there are thousands of big and small e-retailers across these countries. What these e-retailers practice may not be implemented by all e-retailers in the industry. Hence, further research should focus on how small e-retailers protect their e-consumers, and which difficulties they have faced in this aspect, given their size and resource constraints, even though they want to build trust and take care of their e-customers. The next chapter, the conclusion, will summarize what has been discussed in the previous chapters.

References

A Malek, N.H. 2020. "Zalora Still Records Customer Growth this Raya Season." *The Malaysian Reserve,* June 16, 2020.

AsiaOne. 2014. "Singapore Online Retailer Refutes Claim that 900k Customer Accounts Breached." *AsiaOne.* November 12, 2014. https://asiaone.com/digital/singapore-online-retailer-refutes-claim-900k-customer-accounts-breached

Baharudin, H. 2020. "Shopee and Lazada Remove Listings of Unauthorized Microsoft software." *The New Paper,* 28 July 2020. https://tnp.sg/news/singapore/shopee-and-lazada-remove-listings-unauthorised-microsoft-software

Barker, S. 2017. "Lazada Group ups DDoS Protection for its Online Shopping Network." *Security Brief,* June 9, 2017. https://securitybrief.asia/story/lazada-group-ups-ddos-protection-its-online-shopping-network

Bryman, A., and E. Bell. 2003. *Business Research Methods*. New York: Oxford University Press.

Do, M. 2019. "Shoppe & Lazada Still Fighting for Top Spot in Southeast Asian E-commerce." *Vietnam Economic Times*, December 6, 2019. https://vneconomictimes.com/article/business/shopee-lazada-still-fighting-for-top-spot-in-southeast-asian-e-commerce

French Chamber Singapore. 2019. *Interview with Franck Vervia, Lazada: Fighting Cybercrime, on the Defence with AI*. Singapore: French Chamber Singapore. https://fccsingapore.com/news/n/news/lazada-fighting-cybercrime-on-the-defence-with-ai.html

Flyvbjerg, B. 2006. "Five Misunderstandings About Case-Study Research." *Qualitative Inquiry* 12, no. 2, 219–245. doi: 10.1177/1077800405284363

Ha, H. 2012. "Online Security and Consumer Protection in E-commerce - An Australian Case." In *Strategic and Pragmatic E-Business: Implications for Future Business Practices* ed. K.M. Rezaul, 217–243. Hershey, PA: IGI Global.

Ha, H. 2013. "Credit Card Use and Risks in the E-Market: A Case Study in Melbourne, Australia." In *E-Marketing in Developed and Developing Countries: Emerging Practices*. eds. H. El-Gohary, and R. Eid, 214–232. USA: IGI Global. doi: 10.4018/978-1-4666-3954-6.ch013

Ha, H. 2017. "Stakeholders' Views on Self-Regulation to Protect Consumers in E-Retailing." *Journal of Electronic Commerce in Organizations* 153, pp. 83–103.

Hancock, D.R., and B. Algozzine. 2006. *Doing Case Study Research: A Practical Guide for Beginning Researchers*. New York, London: Teachers College Press.

Hara, A. 2020. "E-Commerce Titans Step Up Fake Product Fight." *Vietnam Investment Review*, May 21, 2020. https://vir.com.vn/e-commerce-titans-step-up-fake-product-fight-76350.html

How, M. 2019. "Lazada's CEO Allegedly called S'pore Shopper After Failed Purchase Facebook post went viral." *Mothership*, May 06, 2019. https://mothership.sg/2019/05/lazada-ceo-call-shopping-no-refund/

Lazada Group. undated a. *What are the Payment Methods Available?* Singapore: Lazada Group. https://lazada.sg/helpcenter/what-are-the-payment-methods-available-4179.html?spm=a2o42.helpcenter-topic.articles-list.9.69bb4df67w06ZF

Lazada Group. undated b. *Terms and Conditions*. Singapore: Lazada Group. https://lazada.sg/terms-of-use/?spm=a2o42.helpcenter-article.article-content.1.64407bb9f4u723

Lazada Group. 2019a. *Contact*. Singapore: Lazada Group. https://group.lazada.com/en/contacts/

Lazada Group. 2019b. *Privacy Policy*. Singapore: Lazada Group. https://lazada.sg/privacy-policy/?spm=a2o42.11638377.footer_top.15.28032dd1Kb9PMm

Lazada Group. 2019c. *BSI – Certification of Registration.* Singapore: Lazada Group. https://laz-img-cdn.alicdn.com/tfs/TB1GBlUvYH1gK0jSZ FwXXc7aXXa-1062-1488.png

Marketing Magazine 2019–2020. *Winners (PR Awards 2020).* Singapore: *Marketing Magazine.*

Murugiah, S. 2017. "Zalora Says Unaffected by WannaCry Ransomware Outbreak." theedgemarkets.com, May 19, 2017. https://theedgemarkets. com/article/zalora-says-un affected-wannacry-ransomware-outbreak

Pissedconsumer.com. undated. *Lazada Singapore Reviews and Complaints. Pissed Consumer.* https://lazada-singapore.pissedconsumer.com/review.html

Retailnews.asia. 2019. "Lazada Strengthens its Position as Singapore's Top eCommerce Platform with RedMart's Move to the Lazada app." *Retailnews. asia,* 27 Amr 2019. https://retailnews.asia/lazada-strengthens-its-position-as-singapores-top-ecommerce-platform-with-redmarts-move-to-the-lazada-app/

Sachitanand, R. 2020. "Lazada, Shopee called Out for Inflated Pricing on masks, other COVID-19 Gear." *Campaingasia,* March 12, 2020. https:// campaignasia.com/article/lazada-shopee-called-out-for-inflated-pricing-on-masks-other-covid-19-gear/458731

Singapore Business Review. 2019. "Lazada, Shopee are the two Most Used E-Commerce Apps in Southeast Asia." *Singapore Business Review,* March 16, 2020. https://sbr.com.sg/retail/news/lazada-shopee-are-two-most-used-e-commerce-apps-in-southeast-asia

Singapore Economic Development Board. 2016. *Predicting the Future of E-commerce.* Singapore: Singapore Economic Development Board. https:// edb.gov.sg/en/news-and-events/insights/innovation/predicting-the-future-of-e-commerce.html

Singapore Police Force. 2019. *Police Advisory – Beware of Scams Involving Lazada and Shopee.* Singapore: Singapore Police Force. https://police.gov.sg/media-room/news/20191108_others_beware_of_scams_involving_lazada_and_ shopee_lucky_draws

Shopee undated. *Shopee Careers.* Vietnam: Shopee. https://careers.shopee.sg/job-detail/1736/

Statista. 2020. *Leading E-Commerce Platforms in the Movement Control Order (MCO) Period During the COVID-19 Outbreak in Malaysia as at April 2020.* NewYork, NY: Statista.

Tee, K. 2019. "How online fashion retailer Zalora cracked Southeast Asia." *South Morning China Post,* January 17, 2019. https://scmp.com/lifestyle/ fashion-beauty/article/2182389/how-fashion-portal-zalora-blossomed-cracking-southeast-asia

Teh, A. 2017. "Here's How Big Companies Like Lazada, Ninja Van are Tackling Customer Experience in Ecommerce." *Tech in Asia*, Febraury 23, 2017. https://techinasia.com/heres-big-companies-lazada-ninja-van-tackling-customer-experience-ecommerce

The ASEAN Post. 2018. "Unicorns of ASEAN: Lazada." *The ASEAN Post*, June 11, 2018. From https://theaseanpost.com/article/unicorns-asean-lazada

The Straits Times. 2020. "How Alibaba's Lazada turned produce dumped in coronavirus crisis into a business." *The Straits Times*, May 14, 2020. https://straitstimes.com/business/companies-markets/how-alibabas-lazada-turned-produce-dumped-in-coronavirus-crisis-into-a

Van Anh 2019. "Shopee Delays Handling "Ghost" Vendors?" *Vietnam Investment Review*, September 7, 2019. https://vir.com.vn/shopee-delays-handling-ghost-vendors-70393.html

Velder, M.V.D., P. Jansen, and M. Anderson. 2004. *Guide to Management Research Methods*. Malden, Oxford, Carlton: Blackwell Publishing.

VietNamNet. 2019. "Prohibited goods on Lazada and Shopee." *VietNamNet*, February 26, 2019. https://english.vietnamnet.vn/fms/business/218552/prohibited-goods-on-lazada-and-shopee.html

Zalora. 2019. *Zalora Personal Data Protection Policy*. Malaysia: Zalora.

CHAPTER 6

Conclusion: E-Consumer Protection Now and in the Future

Introduction

This chapter summarizes what has been discussed in the previous chapters and the findings from three case studies of Lazada in Singapore, Shopee in Vietnam, and Zalora in Malaysia. It also draws some conclusions that may offer new insights pertaining to e-consumer protection to various groups of stakeholders. E-consumer protection is a complex, multidimensional, and challenging task given the anonymity and the cross-border, speed, and transient nature of e-retailing (Ha 2012, 2017; Ha and Coghill 2008; Ha, Coghill and Maharaj 2009; Ha and McGregor 2013). The nature of e-retailing makes it difficult for e-consumers to identify fraudulent e-retailers and for relevant organizations to take action against them.

Even though different sectors have worked with one another, the current three-sector governance framework, including the public sector, the private sector, and the civil society, does have shortcomings that require a new or modified governance approach to address the existing and ongoing problems associated with e-consumer protection. Given the technical, legal, and human behavior-related nature of the issues of e-consumer protection, it requires various groups of stakeholders to adopt a mixture of legal framework (e.g., legislation, guidelines, and codes of practice), technological measures (e.g., digital seal and certificate), and human behavior-related measures (e.g., education) to address these issues (OECD 2016, 2018, 2019; World Economic Forum 2013, 2019).

Nevertheless, e-consumers are the subjects of e-transactions and the recipients of any policies. Thus, the "four-sector governance framework," including government, e-retailers, civil society organizations (industry and consumer associations), and e-consumers, has been proposed. It emphasizes cooperation among the four sectors. Importantly, the roles of e-consumers in self-protection to facilitate better governance and enhance the effectiveness of regulatory and self-regulatory measures to address e-consumer protection are stressed in the proposed framework. Given the limited ability and capacity of consumers in self-protection, which was evidenced through the number of complaints and disputes, better and effective e-consumer education and strong support from other groups of stakeholders to assist e-consumers to fulfill their responsibilities are required. The incentive for e-consumers to exercise their responsibilities is their desire to enjoy the advantages of e-retailing; and for consumer associations it is the desire to enhance credibility and have a stronger voice in e-consumer issues. The incentive for e-retailers to fulfill their roles is the desire to attract and retain e-consumers via trust and reputation building; and for industry associations it is the desire to protect the interests of the entire industry.

Policy Implications

Several policy implications arise from this work. First, the six issues associated with e-consumers are interrelated and must be addressed simultaneously. Failure to address any one of these issues would seriously compromise e-consumer protection since the violation of one basic consumer right would lead to the breach of many others.

Second, given the increase in cross-border online fraud and complaints, the research findings strengthen the proposition that governance is important in the achievement of the expected outcomes of the policy framework for e-consumer protection (OECD 2013, 2015). Although insufficient good governance is a common problem applicable to almost all industries, it is more serious in e-retailing because consumers have to face different forms of risks, and it is difficult to investigate such risks when they surface. Above all, lack of governance impedes the success of e-retailing by weakening consumer trust and confidence in e-retailing, in government, and in CSOs (Ha 2017; Ha and McGregor 2013). Thus, the issues associated with e-consumer protection must be addressed through specific actions of each governance sector and common responsibilities of all sectors.

Third, although self-regulation has been encouraged, government still plays an important role in e-consumer protection. Consumers and CSOs are more confident in activities of government than self-regulatory measures adopted by e-retailers to protect e-consumers (Ha 2017; Shergold 2016). Even e-retailers need to work closely with the authorities to discharge their duty in e-consumer protection. However, it is impossible for government, by itself, to address the issues associated with e-consumer protection since the rules of e-retailing cannot be made by governments alone. A more focused effort and an integrated approach involving government, e-retailers, industry and consumer associations, and consumers for improving governance and enhancing consumer trust and confidence could facilitate e-consumer protection and the full potential of e-retailing.

Fourth, e-consumers have to play an active role in self-protection. However, many e-consumers may not practice sufficient self-protection when shopping online due to lack of awareness of online risk. Thus, e-consumer education can empower e-consumers with knowledge and understanding to exercise their rights and social responsibilities in e-retailing (Ha and McGregor 2013). Given the multifaceted nature of problems with e-retailing, e-consumer education needs to focus on technical, legal, and human behavioral aspects regarding e-retailing. A single governance sector may not have sufficient resources and expertise to deliver effective e-consumer education. Again, a joint force of all involved parties could increase the success of such educational activities (OECD 2016; World Economic Forum 2017, 2019). Educational programs can also be tailored by the relevant organizations to increase the level of awareness among e-retailers of their social responsibility and the benefits of providing protection to their customers.

Fifth, it is in the interest of e-retailers to provide protection to their customers since protecting their customers means protecting their business. Self-regulation, voluntary guidelines, and codes of practice do not work well without the willingness of e-retailers to comply with such measures. E-retailers need to go beyond what is required by law to gain competitive advantage and rebuild their reputations since e-consumers appeared to have lack of trust in e-retailers (Ha et al. 2009). Thus, this study suggests that e-retailers should practice CSR and address complaints to enhance e-consumer trust and confidence in e-retailers which, in turn, can change consumers' perceptions of the credibility of the e-retailing industry.

Finally, advanced technological applications have been employed by both e-retailers and e-consumers to enjoy the benefits of e-retailing (Ha 2011, 2013a, 2013b). However, cyber wrongdoers also try to make use of high-tech applications to commit offences. It was found that appropriate technological applications can ensure the security of a system. Thus, the use of technology can contribute to enhancing e-consumer protection. A system must be designed in a way that it is both user-friendly and able to prevent and detect online incidents.

Future Research

Governance to address e-consumer protection is a relatively new area of research, especially in ASEAN. Given that both literature and empirical studies on this topic are currently limited, the findings from this work can serve as a preliminary source for further research. The following issues are not exhaustive, but rather are those of most interest and relevance to e-consumer protection.

First, the proposed governance framework could be initially tested in the e-retailing industry. Further modification could be made based on the experiences gained from the pilot tests. Since the proposed framework addresses the generic problems of improving governance, it can be employed in other sectors.

Second, future research could examine the roles of the media in the dissemination of information which could increase the level of awareness of the public. Educational programs via traditional and social media could have more effect on e-consumers since such media channels can create viral content. The media can easily expose offensive cases to the wider audience. Broadcasting unacceptable behavior of unscrupulous e-retailers on the Internet, via self-help and customer review sites, induces e-retailers to behave better and exhibit respect for consumer rights. However, in this approach, care must be taken to avoid legal implications.

Finally, exploration of the motivations and behaviors of e-consumers about not taking precautions to protect themselves from online incidents can also be a subject of future research. Investigation of the types of problems e-consumers have encountered would help consumer educators tailor appropriate educational programs to suit different groups of consumers. Also, at the macro level, many questions present opportunities for further research, such as "Has the failure or the delay to revise laws created issues? Is there any relationship between the culture of a given country and consumer protection in the country? Do international laws and regulations formulated in Western nations fit Eastern nations?"[1]

Concluding Remarks

This final chapter has summarized the entire volume to address the research objectives stated in the introduction. It has reinforced the arguments for the proposed integrated "four-sector governance framework" to address e-consumer protection. This volume suggests that the three-sector governance framework has limited success, although several measures have been implemented to protect e-consumers. Importantly, nonuniform standards and regulations, weak enforcement of laws, and insufficient participation and cooperation among different groups of stakeholders have impacted the effectiveness of the current measures to protect e-consumers. As a result, e-consumers receive different levels of protection from different e-retailers. Finally, e-consumer ignorance about their basic rights, the current measures to protect them, and their lack of awareness of self-protective measures have weakened their ability to protect themselves in the online market.

The application of the proposed "four-sector governance framework" has the potential to address e-consumer protection more effectively. The proposed framework is distinct from the current framework in terms of stronger cooperation among all sectors, the inclusion of e-consumers, and more involvement of e-retailers for a greater consumer confidence and trust in e-retailing.

In conclusion, this study has addressed the knowledge gaps caused by insufficient information and research on governance and e-consumer protection and has achieved its key objectives of improving the understanding of issues associated with governance and e-consumer protection. It has also provided a better insight into how the conventional governance framework can be improved and an avenue for further research on e-consumer protection.

---

[1] The author would like to thank Dr. Stanley Bruce Thomson for his comments and insights.

References

Ha, H. 2012. "Online Security and Consumer Protection in Ecommerce - An Australian Case." In *Strategic and Pragmatic E-Business: Implications for Future Business Practices* ed. K.M. Rezaul. 217–243. Hershey, PA: IGI Global.

Ha, H. 2013a. "Credit Card Use and Risks in the E-Market: A Case Study in Melbourne, Australia." In *E-Marketing in Developed and Developing Countries: Emerging Practices* eds. H. El-Gohary and R. Eid. 214–232. USA: IGI Global.

Ha, H. 2013b. "Credit Card Use and Debt by Female Students - A Case Study in Melbourne, Australia." *Youth Studies Australia* 32, no. 4, Online.

Ha, H. 2017. "Stakeholders' Views on Self-Regulation to Protect Consumers in E-Retailing." *Journal of Electronic Commerce in Organizations* 15, no. 3, pp. 83–103.

Ha, H., and K. Coghill. 2008. "Online Shoppers in Australia: Dealing with Problems." *International Journal of Consumer Studies* 32, no. 1, pp. 5–17.

Ha, H., K. Coghill, and E.A. Maharaj. 2009. "Current Measures to Protect E-consumers' Privacy in Australia." In *Online Consumer Protection: Theories of Human Relativism,* eds. K. Chen and A. Fadlalla, 123150. Hershey, PA: Idea Group, Inc.

Ha, H., and S.L.T. McGregor. 2013. "Role of Consumer Associations in the Governance of E-commerce Consumer Protection." *Journal of Internet Commerce* 12, no. 1, pp. 1–25.

OECD. 2013. "Trust in Government, Policy Effectiveness and the Governance Agenda." In *Government at a Glance 2013.* Paris; OECD.

OECD. 2015. *Industry Self-Regulation: Role and Use in Supporting Consumer Interests.* Paris: OECD.

OECD. 2016. *Consumer Protection in E-commerce: OECD Recommendation.* Paris: OECD.

OECD. 2018. *Toolkit for Protecting Digital Consumers:* A Resource for G20 Policy Makers.

Shergold, P. 2016. "Three Sectors, One Public Purpose." In *The Three Sector Solution: Delivering Public Policy in Collaboration with Not-for-Profits and Business,* eds. J.R. Butcher and D.J. Gilchrist, 23–32. Canberra: ANU Press.

World Economic Forum. 2013. *The Future Role of Civil Society.* Cologny/Geneva: World Economic Forum, and KPMG International.

World Economic Forum. 2017. *Agile Governance Reimagining Policy-making in the Fourth Industrial Revolution.* Cologny/Geneva: World Economic Forum.

World Economic Forum. 2019. *The Global Governance of Online Consumer Protection and E-commerce Building Trust.* Cologny/Geneva: World Economic Forum.

About the Author

Associate Professor **Huong Ha** is Head, Business Programmes, at School of Business, Singapore University of Social Sciences. She has been affiliated with UON Singapore and University of Newcastle, Australia. Her previous positions include dean, director of research and development, deputy course director, chief editor, executive director, business development manager, and so on. She holds a PhD from Monash University (Australia) and a master's degree from National University of Singapore. She was a recipient of a PhD scholarship (Monash University), Temasek scholarship (National University of Singapore), and a scholarship awarded by the United Nations University/International Leadership Academy, and many other scholarships, professional and academic awards, and research-related grants.

She has authored or coedited the following books:

(i) Ha, Huong, Fernando, L. and Mahajan, S. (2019). *Disaster Risk Management: Case Studies in South Asia*. New York: Business Expert Press.

(ii) Ha, Huong, Fernando, L. and Mahajan, S. (2019). *Disaster Risk Management in Agriculture: Case Studies in South Asia*. New York: Business Expert Press.

(iii) Ha, Huong (2018). *Climate Change Management: Special Topics in the Context of Asia*. USA: Business Expert Press.

(iv) Ha, Huong; Fernando, Lalitha and Mahmood, Amir (eds.) (2015). *Strategic Disaster Risk Management in Asia*, Springer.

(v) Ha, Huong (2014). *Change Management for Sustainability*. USA: Business Expert Press.

(vi) Ha, Huong (2014). *Land and Disaster Management Strategies in Asia*. H. Ha (Ed.), Springer.

(vii) Ha, Huong & Dhakal, T. N. (2013), and (v) *Governance Approaches to Mitigation of and Adaptation to Climate Change in Asia*. H. Ha, & T. N. Dhakal (Eds.), Basingstoke: Palgrave Macmillan.

She has published more than 80 journal articles, books, book chapters, conference papers, and articles in encyclopedias. She has been an invited member of (i) the international editorial boards of many international journals/book projects in many countries; (ii) the scientific and/or technical committees of several international conferences in different countries; and (iii) international advisory board of many associations. She has also been a reviewer of peer-reviewed and high-ranking international journals and international conferences.

Index

Concise and Applied Business Books

www.ingramcontent.com/pod-product-compliance
Lightning Source LLC
Chambersburg PA
CBHW061319220326
41599CB00026B/4956